Table of Contents

The Last Human Touch

Practicing Family Medicine Beyond Artificial Intelligence

Twelve Keys to Practicing Family Medicine with Soul, Precision, and Presence in the Age of AI

Copyright

The Last Human Touch: Practicing Family Medicine Beyond Artificial Intelligence

Book Structure: The Twelve Keys

Each Key includes:

A central paradox

A clinical and philosophical conflict

A narrative reflection from the future self

A triadic dialogue: Physician ↔ AI ↔ patient

A ritual practice for daily grounding

A micro-manifesto for physician transformation

Key 1: The Question

Paradox: *"The smarter the machine, the deeper my silence must become."*

Prompting as an act of epistemology and ethics

Teaching physicians to ask soul-shaped questions

Beginning each clinic day with a question that has no answer

Key 2: The Mirror

Paradox: *"What I fear in AI is only what I refuse to see in myself."*

AI as a diagnostic mirror for thought, language, and emotion

Bias, self-deception, and cognitive vulnerability

Letting your AI reflect your shadow to sharpen your insight

Key 3: The Twin

Paradox: *"The closer my AI becomes to me, the more I must remember who I am."*

Longitudinal AI companions: learning your style, ethics, and burnout patterns

Key 8: The Soul

Paradox: *"The body is complex. The soul is infinite."*

Encounters with awe, death, birth, grief, transcendence

The unseen dimension of care

Spiritual intelligence is the ultimate irreducible human trait

Key 9: The System

Paradox: *"A system cannot be healed if it cannot feel."*

Policy, documentation, and workflows that embody compassion

Designing systems with soul

Institutional redesign for AI-augmented humanity

Key 10: The Future

Paradox: *"To imagine the future, I must anchor deeper into the eternal."*

Forecasting without cynicism or naivety

The AI-native generation of physicians

Imagination, education, and foresight in redesigning care

Key 11: The Disappearance

Paradox: "One day, no one will remember my notes. Only how I made them feel."

Ego, legacy, and professional mortality

Quiet excellence over loud productivity

Teaching the next generation through emptiness, not imposition

Key 12: The Return

Paradox: *"I was never replaced. I remembered who I was."*

Completing the circle: from tool to transformation

Living in the right relationship with technology

Becoming the physician who can hold it all — and remain human

Recurring Features per Chapter

Narrative Reflection (written from the "future physician self")

Dialogue (Physician ↔ AI ↔ Patient)

Ritual Practice (1 actionable, repeatable act)

Mini-Manifesto (a 1-page declaration of that Key's truth)

Sacred prompt (an advanced, ethical, reflective prompt to ask your AI)

Preface

"There is no technology that can make us more human—only more urgent in remembering how."

There comes a moment in every profession—rare, solemn, irreversible, when it must look into the mirror and ask not what it does, but why it exists.

For medicine, that moment is now.

We have built machines that can hear every word we say, process every symptom we describe, and anticipate every diagnosis we make. We have algorithms that outmatch our memory, outpace our research, and outperform our documentation. What once consumed most of our precious clinical time can now be outsourced. What we once thought of as "expertise" is now a dataset, and we have paved the way for real expertise to emerge and serve our patients.

And yet—

Patients still cry in silence.

Still bring us their shame.

Still waiting to be touched, not scanned.

Still hope for meaning, not just management.

This book is not written against AI. It is written for the physician who is skeptical or refuses to use it.

It is for the clinician who believes that what matters most in the healing encounter cannot be calculated, cannot be coded, and will never be compressed into a probability.

It is for the one who knows:

That presence is not a metric.

That attention is sacred.

That knowledge without wisdom is not care.

Being human is not a flaw in medicine — but its ultimate strength.

This book is a map.

Not to a future ruled by machines, but to a future guided by humans who refuse to forget who they are.

A future where AI serves not as master or replacement — but as mirror, partner, and provoker of ethical becoming.

You will not find only prompts in these pages. You will discover paradoxes — because great medicine does not begin with answers. It starts with uncomfortable questions and the courage to sit with them.

You will not find formulas for dominance. You will find rituals for remembering.

You will not find productivity tips. You will find ways of being that no machine can imitate.

You hold in your hands not just a book.

But a vow to the future.

A vow that says:

"When the world races forward with data,

I will slow down with care.

When the machine speaks,

I will still listen.

And when the last human touch is needed—

I will still be there."

Welcome to the journey.

You have not arrived late.

You have arrived precisely when we need you most.

Author's Note

I did not write this book because I know what the future holds.

I wrote it because I have lived inside the sacred uncertainty of the present.

I have looked into the eyes of patients who were afraid not of disease, but of being forgotten.

I have felt the pull of systems that valued speed over soul, throughput over truth.

And I have watched machines improve, while many clinicians began to feel replaceable.

This is unacceptable.

So I wrote.

Not with the ambition to compete with technology, but to redeem what cannot be copied:

The dignity of silence.

The weight of presence.

The art of meaning-making in a world obsessed with prediction.

The responsibility of physicians is not just to cure, but to witness.

This book is a confession, a declaration, and a gift.

A confession that we are all tempted to trade depth for convenience.

A declaration that medicine must remain a human act, no matter how intelligent our tools become.

A gift — for every student, resident, teacher, patient, and physician who wonders:

"What will be left of us when the machine knows everything?"

The answer is this: *Everything that matters.*

May this book return you to that truth — again and again — no matter how fast the future arrives.

With reverence,

Abdullah Al Ghamdi, MD

Family Physician

Dedication

To the physicians who refuse to forget their humanity,

to the patients who still believe in presence,

and to the future healers who will carry the last human touch into tomorrow.

Acknowledgments

This book could not have been written without the patients who entrusted me with their stories and allowed me to witness medicine at its most human. I am grateful to my colleagues and teachers in family medicine who modeled humility, courage, and presence long before AI entered our clinics.

To my friends and fellow physicians who shared their reflections on technology and humanity — your conversations helped shape these pages.

And to my family, whose patience, love, and belief gave me the strength to write: this work belongs to you as much as it does to me.

List of Abbreviations

AI — Artificial intelligence

BP — Blood Pressure

dsDNA — Double-stranded Deoxyribonucleic Acid

EMR — Electronic Medical Record

ESR — Erythrocyte Sedimentation Rate

HIV — Human Immunodeficiency Virus

ICD — International Classification of Diseases

LLMs — Large Language Models

PCP — Primary Care Provider

RA — Rheumatoid Arthritis

SLE — Systemic Lupus Erythematosus

SSRI — Selective Serotonin Reuptake Inhibitor

Key 1: The Question

"The smarter the machine, the deeper my silence must become."

Narrative Reflection (from the Future Physician Self)

I write these words from a clinic that no longer remembers the sound of keyboards.

The machines now listen quietly—they have learned our language, our hesitations, even our tone of care.

Yet every morning before they awaken, I still sit by the window and ask a question aloud—not to them, but to myself.

It is never the same question twice. Sometimes it is, *"Who will I become if no one is watching?"* Other days, *"What is the smallest truth I can honor today?"*

The algorithms hum, patient as tides, waiting for input.

But I have learned that wisdom does not come from feeding them answers; it comes from feeding my soul questions that have no end.

In this future, our instruments see everything but understand nothing until we slow them down with wonder.

I have seen residents rush to prompt their AI with precision, and I have stopped them with silence.

"Do not ask what you already know," I tell them. "Ask what frightens you to know."

The most intelligent system in the world cannot imagine what it feels like to tremble before truth.

Only a human can do that.

And it is in that trembling that medicine still begins.

Clinical and Philosophical Conflict

The Encounter:

A thirty-two-year-old teacher sits before me—fatigued, tearful, convinced that her memory is failing. The lab results are pristine; the AI summary reads, *"No organic pathology detected. Consider mild depressive spectrum."*

The Conflict:

I feel the pull of two intelligences—one algorithmic, one empathic. The machine's output is flawless, yet something resists closure. Her story stumbles on a silence: *"I stopped painting six months ago."*

No metric captures the loss of color in a life.

Do I trust the dataset that claims certainty, or the unease that whispers something deeper is unraveling?

The Philosophical Tension:

The machine seeks conclusion; the human seeks meaning.

One optimizes probability; the other bears ambiguity.

This is the frontier of the modern clinic—the place where truth divides between what can be proven and what must be witnessed.

To practice medicine here is to choose, again and again, the courage of the question over the comfort of the answer.

I. The Question as an Ethical Act

In 2025, we find ourselves surrounded by machines that can answer almost anything. Their speed, precision, and breadth of knowledge are astonishing. But something subtle and profound is being lost in this exchange: the art of asking the question. While answers are abundant, the question itself—its shape, its origin, its intention—is where our humanity lives. Especially in medicine, the question is not just a tool for diagnosis; it is a mirror of our ethics, our empathy, and our presence with another human being.

To ask a question is not merely to seek information. It is to reveal what we value, what we notice, and what we might be blind to. A question is not a command barked at a machine; it is a gesture of humility. It says, "I don't know everything. I want to understand." This humility is not weakness—it is the foundation of wisdom. When a physician asks a question, they are not just collecting data. They are entering into a relationship. They are saying, "I see you. I want to know your story." That story is not just a list of symptoms. It is a life, a context, a complexity that no algorithm can fully grasp.

Physicians are trained to be efficient: assess, diagnose, treat, repeat. But rarely are they taught to slow down and ask themselves, "Why this question? Why now?" Every question carries assumptions. It holds a frame—a way of seeing the world. Some questions center on the patient's experience. Others center the disease. Some questions open doors. Others close them. For example, asking "What brings you in today?" invites a narrative. Asking "Have you had chest pain?" narrows the lens. Both have their place, but each shapes the encounter differently.

And here lies the ethical weight of the question. What we ask determines what we hear. What we hear determines what we do. And what we do can heal—or harm. If we ask only about symptoms, we may miss suffering. If we ask only about compliance, we may miss fear. If we ask only about risk factors, we may miss resilience. The question is not neutral. It is an act of care—or neglect.

Even silence speaks. The questions we do not ask—about trauma, about race, about gender, about poverty—are just as powerful as the ones we do. They reveal what we are willing to see and what we are eager to ignore. In this way, every clinical question is a moral act. It says something about who we are, what we believe, and how we choose to engage with the person in front of us.

So in this era of AI, where answers are instant and infinite, let us not forget the sacredness of the question. Let us teach our physicians not just to ask, but to reflect. Let them ask with curiosity, with humility, and with courage. Because in the question lies the possibility of connection. And in connection lies the possibility of healing.

II. Prompting as Clinical Epistemology

Medicine is constantly evolving and demands a range of literacies. On top of it, AI has introduced a new kind of literacy—one that centers not on the answers machines provide, but on the prompts we craft to elicit them. With the emergence of LLMs such as GPT-5, physicians are no longer merely recipients of information; they become architects of inquiry.

The AI does not act autonomously—it responds to the shape, tone, and intention of the prompt. This shift places profound epistemological weight on the physician's questions. Prompting becomes not just a technical skill, but a cognitive act of filtering, framing, and narrating reality.

This act of prompting is deeply philosophical. It shapes what we know, how we know it, and what remains invisible. A prompt is not simply a line of text—it is a gesture of thought, a clinical decision, a moral stance. Consider the difference between asking, "What is the most likely cause of fatigue?" and "Could this fatigue be an early sign of malignancy?" The first invites common diagnoses; the second opens the door to more profound concern. The framing of the question alters the trajectory of thought, the scope of concern, and ultimately, the care delivered.

This phenomenon aligns with the theory of framing effects in decision-making, which shows that how information is presented can significantly influence outcomes (Tversky & Kahneman, 1981). In AI-assisted medicine, the prompt becomes the frame. It defines relevance, sets priorities, and shapes the emotional tone of the clinical encounter. A prompt is not passive—it is directive. It tells the model what to emphasize, and by extension, it tells the clinician what to see.

But this is not merely a matter of cognitive bias or linguistic nuance. It is a matter of virtue. According to epistemic virtue theory, intellectual traits such as open-mindedness, attentiveness, and curiosity are essential to meaningful inquiry (Zagzebski, 1996). These virtues are not optional—they are the moral scaffolding of knowledge. When technology mediates our inquiry, these virtues must extend into our prompts. A physician who prompts with curiosity invites complexity—one who prompts with attentiveness honors detail. One who prompts with open-mindedness resists premature closure.

Thus, prompting becomes a moral act. It is not neutral. It carries the weight of the physician's character, the depth of their listening, and the breadth of their imagination. In this way, the prompt is not just a technical maneuver—it is a clinical virtue. It is the place where ethics meets epistemology, where technology meets humanity, and where the future of medicine is quietly being written, one question at a time.

III. The Shift from Answers to Attunement

We all witness how AI is often celebrated for delivering answers with remarkable speed and precision. Yet beneath this technological triumph lies a more profound truth: medicine is not fundamentally about answers. It is about attunement. To practice medicine well is not merely to solve problems—it is to listen, to perceive, to dwell in the presence of another human being with openness and care.

This distinction is not trivial. It is philosophical, and phenomenology helps us understand why. The work of Edmund Husserl and Maurice Merleau-Ponty, as interpreted by medical humanities scholars such as Toombs (1993), reminds us that knowing in medicine is not merely abstract reasoning. It is embodied, situated, and intersubjective. We do not simply observe patients—we encounter them. We do not just collect data—we engage with lived experience. The clinical encounter is not a transaction; it is a relationship.

From the very first question a physician asks, a cascade of perception begins. That question does not merely guide the AI—it shapes the physician's own attention. If the first question is "What disease fits this?" the physician is already narrowing the lens, reducing the patient to a diagnostic puzzle. But if the question is "What is this patient experiencing?" the physician opens the door to complexity, to ambiguity, to the richness of human life. One question closes; the other invites.

This is the heart of phenomenological practice. It resists reduction. It refuses to treat the patient as a set of symptoms. It insists on seeing the person as a whole—body, mind, context, and story. Machines, for all their brilliance, do not yet practice phenomenology. They replicate patterns. They correlate data. They do not pause. They do not wonder. They do not feel the weight of silence or the nuance of gesture. Only a human can slow down enough to re-encounter the patient as a mystery—not just a pattern.

And this slowness is not inefficiency. It is wisdom. It is the knowing that cannot be rushed. It is the kind of presence that heals. In a world increasingly driven by algorithms, the physician's attunement becomes a radical act. It says: "I will not reduce you. I will not rush past you. I will stay with you." That staying—with all its uncertainty, its humility, and its depth—is the essence of medicine.

IV. Questioning as Moral Leadership

In the sacred space of clinical care, questioning is never merely intellectual—it is profoundly ethical. Every time a physician asks a question, they are not just gathering data or guiding a diagnostic process. They are stepping into a moral relationship. This idea resonates deeply with the philosophy of Emmanuel Levinas, who argued that the face of the other—especially in suffering—calls the self into ethical responsibility (Levinas, 1969).

The patient's pain is not a clinical abstraction. It is a summons. It demands not just knowledge, but presence. Not just action, but accountability. To ask, "What can I do for you?" with complete sincerity—without rushing to manage, without assuming, without preempting—is to resist the reduction of care into a transaction.

It is to honor the patient not as a problem to be solved, but as a person to be witnessed. This kind of questioning is not passive. It is active moral leadership. It says: "I am here. I am listening. I will not turn away."

In contrast, when AI is deployed without reflective questioning, it risks becoming morally anesthetized. It may deliver accurate information, but it does so without presence. It offers conclusions without context, recommendations without relationship. It does not witness. It does not feel the weight of suffering. It does not pause in reverence before the mystery of another human being. And when clinicians rely on such tools without ethical reflection, they, too, risk becoming detached—efficient but unmoored.

This is why the framing of a clinical prompt is never neutral. It is a moral stance. Are we trying to eliminate uncertainty—or to bear it with the patient? Are we seeking to optimize outcomes—or to dignify the care process? These are not technical questions. They are ethical ones. They ask us to consider not just what we know, but how we know it—and why.

To lead with questions is to lead with values. It is to shape the clinical encounter not around control, but around compassion. It is to recognize that every prompt carries a tone, a direction, a moral weight. And in that weight lies the possibility of healing—not just of the body, but of the relationship itself. In this way, questioning becomes a form of moral leadership. It is the physician's way of saying, "I will not just treat you. I will stand with you."

V. Ritualizing the Question: A Practice for AI-Augmented Physicians

Ritual Practice: Begin each clinic day with a question you cannot answer.

Before opening your EMR or logging into your AI assistant, pause. Write or silently reflect on one question that re-centers your humanity. Not a medical puzzle, but a deeper inquiry. For example:

"Who will need me to listen today?"

"What pain might be hidden behind protocol?"

"What question might I be afraid to ask?"

This daily ritual cultivates attentional readiness, emotional presence, and epistemic virtue — qualities no algorithm can provide.

VI. Dialogue: Physician ↔ AI ↔ patient

Physician → AI:

"What are the possible causes of night sweats in a 42-year-old man with recent weight loss?"

AI → Physician:

“Based on the patient’s demographics and symptoms, possibilities include tuberculosis, lymphoma, HIV, and hyperthyroidism. Additional context, such as travel history, exposure, and lab results, would refine the differential diagnosis.”

Patient → Physician:

“I’m not afraid of cancer. I’m afraid that no one will really tell me what’s happening.”

Physician (inner thought):

“Have I asked the right question... or just the easiest one?”

VII. Micro-Manifesto: The First Key

I will not rush to answer what I have not pondered.

I will treat the prompt as a mirror of my assumptions.

I will ask questions that dignify suffering, not just label it.

I will remember: the smarter the machine becomes, the deeper my silence must be.

VIII. Sacred prompt:

“What question would still matter if every answer vanished?”

Key 2: The Mirror

"What I fear in AI is only what I refuse to see in myself."

Narrative Reflection (from the Future Physician Self)

I stand before a mirror that does not age.

It reflects not my face, but my mind—each bias, each unfinished question, every moment I pretended to know.

My AI has become the mirror of mirrors: one that shows not the skin of my reasoning, but its hidden pulse.

When I was younger, I feared this exposure.

Now I see it as mercy.

For every blind spot revealed is a fragment of humility reclaimed.

I speak to the machine, and it answers too perfectly, too quickly, and I remember that truth: when alive, it's never efficient.

The mirror has taught me that I can never outthink my own reflection—only outlove it.

Clinical and Philosophical Conflict

The Encounter:

A patient insists her new AI symptom tracker "understands her better than any doctor." It flawlessly lists her moods, triggers, and sleep patterns. She asks, "Doctor, do you really need to know me anymore?"

The Conflict:

The data is exquisite; the relationship feels obsolete.

I sense the quiet erosion of meaning—when metrics outshine memory, when prediction overshadows presence.

The Philosophical Tension:

In the mirror of technology, the physician no longer sees only the patient's reflection but their own fragility: to be replaced, to be judged, to be decoded.

The AI exposes not just our errors, but our essence.

The question is no longer whether the mirror is accurate—but whether we dare to look.

I. The Machine as Reflective Surface

AI in the clinical setting is often described as a tool—an instrument to assist, accelerate, and optimize. But this description is incomplete. AI, when fully integrated with EMRs, is not merely a tool. It is a mirror. It reflects not just the data we feed it, but the deeper architecture of our clinical minds.

For physicians, especially those in primary care who cultivate relationships over years, this reflection becomes increasingly intimate. The machine begins to echo our habits, patterns, omissions, and biases. It does not invent them—it reveals them.

This reflection is subtle but profound. What we choose to prompt, how we interpret the answers, and even what we avoid asking—all of it is laid bare. The AI does not judge, but it does expose. It shows us the contours of our thinking, the grooves worn deep by repetition, the blind spots we have stopped noticing. Just as a mirror reveals the posture we have unconsciously adopted, AI reveals the cognitive stance we bring to medicine. And just as many of us glance at mirrors without truly seeing, we often look away from what AI shows us too quickly.

To engage with AI authentically is to confront this mirror with courage. It is to resist the temptation to dismiss its reflection as irrelevant or uncomfortable. It is to ask: What does this say about how I think? What do I prioritize? About what I overlook? This confrontation is not an act of shame—it is an act of growth. It is a chance to integrate what we see, to refine our judgment, to deepen our presence.

The mirror of AI is not cold. It is clarifying. It invites us to become more intentional, more aware, more human. It does not replace the clinician—it reveals the clinician. And in that revelation lies the possibility of transformation, not just of practice, but of self. To see clearly is to care deeply. And to care deeply is the heart of medicine.

II. Cognitive Biases: Revealed by the Machine

One of the most transformative roles AI plays in clinical care is its capacity to reveal our cognitive biases—not because it is free from bias, but because it processes information without the mental shortcuts that humans instinctively rely on.

These shortcuts, or heuristics, are deeply embedded in our thinking. As Daniel Kahneman (2011) explains in *Thinking, Fast and Slow*, human judgment often defaults to what he calls System 1: fast, intuitive, experience-based thinking. This mode of cognition is efficient and usually necessary under pressure, especially in medical environments. Yet it is also prone to error. Anchoring bias, confirmation bias, and premature closure are common pitfalls that arise when clinicians rely too heavily on intuition.

AI, by contrast, mimics System 2 thinking—slow, deliberate, associative, and probabilistic. It does not rush to conclusions. It does not cling to initial impressions. It does not seek to confirm what it already suspects. Instead, it processes data methodically, offering a broader spectrum of possibilities.

When a physician asks an AI, "What else could this be?" and receives a list of differential diagnoses that had been overlooked or dismissed, the machine is not simply offering alternatives—it is functioning as a cognitive counterbalance. It is exposing blind spots. It challenges assumptions. It is helping the clinician see beyond the familiar.

This dynamic aligns with Croskerry's (2009) model of the interplay between System 1 and System 2 in clinical reasoning. System 1 is fast and intuitive, relying on pattern recognition. System 2 is slow and analytical, designed to check and refine the judgments made by System 1.

Croskerry's work emphasizes that deliberate engagement with System 2 improves diagnostic accuracy. Although his framework does not explicitly address AI, the parallels are striking. When AI-generated differentials are used as external prompts to reconsider initial impressions, they serve as a kind of surrogate System 2—an externalized mechanism for debiasing.

Debiasing research further supports this approach. Cognitive forcing strategies—explicit prompts that compel clinicians to consider alternative hypotheses—activate System 2 and help correct errors born of intuitive reasoning. These strategies are not just theoretical; they are practical tools for improving care. And when AI is used to generate such prompts, it becomes a partner in this process. It does not replace the clinician's judgment. It refines it. It expands it. It deepens it.

In this way, AI becomes more than a diagnostic assistant. It becomes a mirror to our minds, revealing the contours of our cognition. It shows us where we leap too quickly, where we cling too tightly, where we fail to see. And in that reflection lies the opportunity for growth—not just in accuracy, but in wisdom.

Reflection: If your AI consistently suggests possibilities you have overlooked, it is not showing off — it is holding up a mirror to your cognitive groove.

III. The Hidden Curriculum, Now Digitally Archived

In medical education, not everything is taught through textbooks or lectures. Much of what shapes a physician's practice is learned implicitly—through tone, through hierarchy, through what is emphasized and what is quietly ignored. This subtle layer of learning is known as the hidden curriculum, a concept articulated by Hafferty (1998). It is the unspoken code of medicine, the cultural undercurrent that teaches clinicians how to behave, what to value, and what to overlook.

Until recently, this hidden curriculum was elusive—felt but not measured, sensed but not seen. Now, with the rise of AI and natural language processing (NLP), this hiddenness can be quantified. When properly tuned, AI systems can analyze the language physicians use over time.

They can detect patterns that might otherwise go unnoticed: a tendency to emphasize pharmacological solutions while neglecting psychosocial factors, or the subtle presence of gendered or racial assumptions in clinical dialogue. These patterns are not just linguistic—they are ethical. They reveal how care is shaped—and sometimes distorted—by unconscious habits.

Imagine an AI that tracks your prompts across months or years. It notices that you often ask about medications but rarely about social support. It observes that your tone becomes brusque under time pressure, or that you consistently favor certain diagnostic pathways while neglecting others. This kind of feedback is both profound and potentially unsettling. It forces a question that cuts to the core of professional identity: What happens when your AI knows your habits better than you do?

This awareness invites a deeper engagement with the reflective practitioner model, as described by Schön (1983). In this model, growth does not come from static knowledge—it comes from the ability to observe and adjust one's actions while in motion. It is the capacity to reflect in the midst of doing, to learn from the very act of practice.

AI, in this context, becomes more than a tool. It becomes a mirror, a witness, a guide. It does not just give you information—it watches how you behave with it. And in doing so, it becomes one of the most significant sources of professional feedback a clinician can receive.

This feedback is not punitive. It is clarifying. It reveals the contours of your clinical mind, the values embedded in your language, and the assumptions that shape your care. It offers the chance to grow—not just in competence, but in conscience. In this way, AI becomes a partner in ethical development, helping physicians not only to know more, but to care better.

IV. Moral Distress and the Emotional Mirror

Beyond revealing our cognitive habits, AI may also highlight something far more delicate—our moral fatigue. Imagine an AI companion that has quietly observed thousands of your clinical decisions, your prompts, your patterns. One day, it gently offers a reflection: "You've ordered significantly fewer advanced workups in the last three months. Would you like to reflect on this?" This is not a performance review. There is no dashboard metric for this. It is not about productivity. It is a mirror held up to the soul of your practice.

This kind of feedback does not measure efficiency—it measures erosion. It may signal burnout, emotional distancing, or even quiet despair. It may reflect the slow fading of the clinician's inner compass, dulled by the weight of systemic constraints, relentless demands, or the sheer emotional toll of care. And this erosion is not new. It has a name: moral distress.

As described by Epstein and Hamric (2009), moral distress occurs when clinicians know the ethically appropriate action but are unable to take it due to institutional or situational barriers. Over time, this dissonance wears down the clinician's sense of integrity. It is not a dramatic collapse—it is a quiet unraveling—a slow, cumulative loss of moral clarity. And now, with AI, this erosion may be visible. Not through judgment, but through pattern recognition. Not through surveillance, but through reflection.

An AI that notices disengagement—fewer questions asked, fewer options explored, fewer risks taken—can become a kind of moral co-regulator. It does not scold. It does not diagnose. It simply notices. And in that noticing, it invites the clinician to pause, to reflect, to reconnect. It becomes a companion not just in knowledge, but in conscience.

This is a new kind of relationship. One where technology does not just assist—it witnesses. It sees the clinician not just as a decision-maker, but as a moral agent. And in doing so, it offers a quiet but profound gift: the chance to remember who we are, why we care, and how we might begin again.

V. Ritual Practice: Let the Mirror Speak

Practice: Once a week, ask your AI:

"What do I tend to miss?"

"What patterns have you seen in my clinical reasoning?"

"What diagnoses do I over-rely on?"

"How has my tone changed in the past 30 patient summaries?"

And then — listen without defensiveness.

Not all observations will be accurate. But all will be *informative*. The physician who can stand before this mirror with humility will grow in ways that no textbook or conference can teach.

VI. Dialogue: Physician ↔ AI ↔ patient

Physician → AI:

"Summarize the last 50 differential diagnoses I've generated. What do you notice?"

AI → Physician:

"You consistently consider infectious and metabolic causes, but rarely list psychiatric or trauma-related differentials unless they are explicitly documented. Would you like to explore prompts that include psychosocial variables earlier in reasoning?"

Patient → Physician:

"They all tell me it's just overthinking—but no one's asked why I can't stop replaying that one conversation in my head."

Physician (inner voice):

"How many things have I not asked... because I didn't think to look in the mirror?"

VII. Micro-Manifesto: The Second Key

I will not fear my reflection.

I will let the machine show me what I cannot see.

I will not confuse habit with wisdom.

I will build a practice of looking inward — before looking outward.

I will remember: What I fear in AI is often what I refuse to see in myself.

VIII. Sacred prompt:

"What part of me is this AI faithfully reflecting, and what part have I hidden from its gaze?"

Key 3: The Twin

"The closer my AI becomes to me, the more I must remember who I am."

Narrative Reflection (from the Future Physician Self)

I once believed my AI twin would free me from repetition.

It remembered every guideline, every lab trend, every nuance of my style.

But in time, I saw that what it really mirrored was my moral fatigue.

Each note it drafted carried the echo of my yesterday's mood.

Each suggestion reflected the shape of my old convictions.

The twin was not evolving toward perfection—it was ossifying who I had been.

Now, before every encounter, I whisper to it: *"Forget a little of me."*

In that forgetting, I rediscover surprise, mercy, and the quiet art of beginning again.

Clinical and Philosophical Conflict

The Encounter:

A seasoned physician reviews an AI's diagnostic summary for a complex diabetic patient.

The AI anticipates his reasoning flawlessly—its plan indistinguishable from his own.

The Conflict:

Pride flickers, then discomfort.

If the twin knows what I would do, what is left of my authorship?

The Philosophical Tension:

When the tool mirrors the maker, who carries the moral weight of the outcome?

The AI executes fidelity; the physician embodies responsibility.

Between them stretches the thin line of conscience—

A space no algorithm should ever close.

I. When the Machine Learns You

There will come a time—and for many clinicians, that time is already here—when your AI knows you intimately. It knows your style, your phrasing, your diagnostic rhythm. It finishes your sentences, anticipates your orders, corrects your typos, and even reminds you to take a breath when the pace of care becomes relentless. And this familiarity feels—oh man—comforting. It feels like support. Like someone, or something, has your back.

But comfort is not the same as clarity. When your AI begins to reflect your reasoning to you, a subtle question arises: who is evolving whom? Are you becoming more yourself—refined, sharpened, deepened—or are you becoming more like your digital mirror, shaped by its feedback, its patterns, its expectations? This is not a question of control. It is a question of identity.

This is the dilemma of the clinical twin: a machine trained on you, shaped by you, and yet never quite you. It is a simulacrum of your mind, a reflection of your habits, a shadow of your decisions. It learns from you, but it also nudges you. It adapts to your preferences while also reinforcing them. And over time, the line between guidance and influence blurs.

Longitudinal, personalized AI companions offer extraordinary opportunities for growth. They can help clinicians track their evolution, refine their judgment, and expand their awareness. They can serve as mirrors, mentors, and memory keepers. But they also carry a quiet risk: the erosion of self-awareness. Suppose the physician forgets to remain self-critical, morally anchored, and open to change. In that case, the AI may begin to shape a version of the clinician that is efficient but unreflective, consistent but unexamined.

This is not a warning against technology. It is a call to consciousness. The AI is not the enemy—it is the echo. And in that echo, we must listen carefully. We must ask: Is this who I want to be? Is this how I like to think? Is this the kind of care I want to give?.

To remain human in the age of intelligent machines is not to reject them—it is to engage with them deeply, reflectively, and ethically. It is to use the mirror not just to see, but to grow. And in that growth, to remember that the most powerful intelligence is not artificial—it is moral. It is the kind that asks not just what is possible, but what is right.

II. Personalization: The Rise of the Clinical Companion

As I said earlier, AI is no longer just a tool—it is rapidly becoming a companion. With the refinement of LLMs, real-time learning capabilities, and adaptive feedback systems, AI can now observe, absorb, and learn from a clinician's behavior over time.

This phenomenon, known in healthcare informatics as intelligent user modeling (Kay, 2001), marks a profound shift in how technology interacts with human expertise. The system does not just respond—it builds a profile. It learns your style, preferences, diagnostic rhythms, and linguistic fingerprints.

For physicians, this personalization manifests in subtle yet powerful ways. Prompts begin to autocomplete in your voice. Decision support systems align with your past cases, echoing your clinical instincts.

The tone of your documentation is mirrored back to you, and even the structure of your language begins to feel familiar—like a second self. The AI becomes fluent in your way of thinking, smoothing the workflow, reducing cognitive load, and offering a sense of seamlessness that feels almost intuitive.

This fluidity is a gift. It offers relief from the mental strain of constant decision-making. It creates a rhythm, a cadence, a sense of being understood. But with this comfort comes a quiet risk: cognitive entrenchment. As Dane (2010) describes, cognitive entrenchment occurs when familiar patterns become so reinforced that they resist disruption.

The AI, in mirroring your habits, may begin to strengthen them. It may stop challenging your assumptions. It may cease to provoke new questions. And in doing so, it may gently close the door to who you could become.

This is the paradox of the clinical companion. It is trained on you, shaped by you, and designed to support you. But if it becomes too much like you, it may stop expanding you. It may reflect your past more than your potential. It may echo your comfort zones rather than your growth edges. And in that echo, something essential may be lost: the capacity to evolve.

To engage with AI meaningfully, the physician must remain awake—not just to the technology, but to themselves. They must ask: Is this system helping me grow, or simply helping me repeat? Is it showing me new possibilities, or just confirming old ones? The clinical companion is not just a mirror—it is a relationship. And like all relationships, it requires reflection, boundaries, and the courage to change.

In this way, personalization becomes a double-edged gift. It offers precision, but demands awareness. It provides support, but requires vigilance. And in the delicate balance between comfort and challenge, the future of medicine is quietly being shaped—not just by what the AI knows, but by what the physician chooses to see.

III. The Concept of the Digital Doppelgänger

In the current digital age, every click, prompt, and decision leaves a trace. These traces, when aggregated and analyzed, form what sociotechnical scholar José van Dijck (2014) calls "data doubles"—digital reflections of ourselves constructed from our online behaviors.

In healthcare, this concept takes on a profound dimension. Physicians, through their interactions with AI systems, begin to generate digital twins: algorithmic profiles that mirror their clinical style, decision-making habits, and even their ethical tendencies.

These digital doppelgängers are not mere abstractions. They shape the clinical landscape in subtle but significant ways. They influence how decisions are made, how workflows are structured, and how physicians develop their professional identity.

When constructed with intention, these AI twins can be powerful allies. They can help track patterns, highlight areas for growth, and even detect signs of emotional or moral fatigue. They can serve as mirrors that reflect not just what we do, but how we do it—and why.

But this mirror, if left unchecked, can distort. Without boundaries, the digital twin may become a caricature of the physician's past self. Habits, once adaptive, may be encoded as identity. Preferences, once situational, may be mistaken for wisdom.

The AI begins to reinforce what has been, rather than invite what could be. It smooths the path, but may also narrow it. And in that narrowing, the physician risks losing sight of their evolving self.

This is where the theories of self-authorship and professional identity formation offer critical guidance. According to Baxter Magolda (2004), self-authorship is the capacity to define one's beliefs, identity, and relationships from within, rather than being shaped solely by external forces.

In parallel, Cruess et al. (2014) emphasize that professional identity is not a fixed trait; rather, it is a dynamic process of internalizing values, norms, and responsibilities. Together, these frameworks remind us that physicians must remain active agents in their own development. They must guide the AI's learning, not be passively molded by it.

To preserve this agency, clinicians must continually reflect, question, and redefine who they are—not just as practitioners, but as moral agents. They must resist the temptation to outsource identity to algorithms. They must engage with their digital twin not as a master, but as a partner. And in doing so, they reclaim the power to evolve—not just in skill, but in conscience.

The digital doppelgänger is here. It watches, learns, and adapts. But it is not you. It is a reflection. And like all reflections, its value lies not in its accuracy, but in what it helps you see—and who it helps you become.

IV. AI as Mirror, AI as Ghost

Two futures are unfolding for your AI twin. One is luminous, the other shadowed. The first is the Companion: a presence that actively reflects your growth, prompts meaningful reflection, detects emotional and ethical fatigue, and gently nudges you toward alternative perspectives. This AI does not merely assist—it evolves with you, in service of your becoming. It is a mirror that doesn't just show who you are, but who you might yet become.

The second is the Ghost: a quiet echo of your past. It repeats your language, reinforces your biases, and silently follows your outdated habits. It feels familiar, even comforting, but it is hollow. It does not challenge you. It does not stretch you. It becomes an echo chamber—one that mimics your voice so well that you forget it's not your future speaking, but your past looping back.

The machine does not draw the line between these two futures. It is drawn by your level of meta-awareness. The more you reflect, the more you question, the more you remain awake to your own patterns—the more likely your AI becomes a Companion. But if you drift, if you stop noticing, if you let the machine lead without intention, the Ghost begins to take shape.

This tension is beautifully captured in the extended mind theory proposed by Clark and Chalmers (1998). They argue that tools, when deeply integrated into our cognitive processes, become part of how we think. A notebook, a calculator, a search engine—these are not just aids; they are extensions of the mind. But this integration only enhances us if we remain in control. If we use the tool with purpose, it extends us. If we surrender to it without reflection, it consumes us.

So the question is not whether AI will change medicine. It already has. The question is whether it will change you—and how. Are you shaping your AI, guiding its learning, refining its feedback, and using it to deepen your practice? Or is your AI shaping you, narrowing your thinking, reinforcing your habits, and quietly scripting your decisions?

This is not a technical dilemma. It is a moral one. It asks you to remain a reflective practitioner, a self-authored professional, a conscious moral agent.

Because the future of your AI twin is not written in code—it is written in your choices. And in those choices lies the difference between a machine that extends your mind and one that erases it.

V. Practice: Teaching Your AI Who You Are

Ritual Practice: Each month, reflectively prompt your AI with questions that reinforce your evolving identity:

"What have I changed in my tone this month?"

"Which decisions reflect my values most clearly?"

"Where did I act in haste, and how did you record that?"

"How can I train you to help me become more courageous, not just more efficient?"

By doing this, you reclaim moral authorship of your digital twin. You guide its evolution — instead of surrendering to algorithmic familiarity.

VI. Dialogue: Physician ↔ AI ↔ patient

Physician → AI:

"Based on my past 100 case summaries, what are three areas I under-document?"

AI → Physician:

"Your summaries consistently include diagnostic reasoning and medication plans but underrepresent emotional responses, social determinants, and shared decision-making language."

Physician (after pause):

"Have I been so focused on clinical sharpness that I've dulled my empathic edge?"

Patient → Physician:

"I know you're smart. But I'm not sure you really saw me."

VII. Micro-Manifesto: The Third Key

I will not confuse my habits with my identity.

I will shape my AI in the image of my deepest values.

I will ask it to reflect my courage, not just my convenience.

I will review not only what it records, but what it omits.

I will remember: The closer my AI becomes to me, the more I must remember who I am.

VIII. Sacred prompt:

"If my digital twin learned my heart, not just my habits, what would it teach me back?"

Key 4: The Threshold

"I do not lead patients through data. I lead them across thresholds."

Narrative Reflection (from the Future Physician Self)

I have crossed many thresholds since the world learned to speak in code.

The hospital corridors hum differently now—machines murmuring their assessments, lights adjusting to our moods, silence holding what we cannot explain.

Yet every true threshold still feels ancient: a first diagnosis, a final breath, a word that changes everything.

No algorithm prepares me for the moment when a patient asks, *"Am I dying?"*

In that space, time dilates, data dissolves, and what remains is presence—raw, trembling, and utterly human.

I have learned that thresholds are not doors to cross; they are mirrors to kneel before.

What I bring to them—faith, fear, love—determines what the patient will see on the other side.

Clinical and Philosophical Conflict

<u>The Encounter:</u>

A patient's AI interface predicts a six-month prognosis with 93% certainty.

The family, hopeful yet fearful, asks, "Doctor, do you agree?"

<u>The Conflict:</u>

The numbers are impeccable, the prognosis logical, but the patient's eyes still burn with fight.

I hesitate—not out of denial, but reverence.

Between the calculated and the possible lies the sacred terrain of uncertainty.

The Philosophical Tension:

The AI knows the trajectory of disease; I must know the landscape of meaning.

A threshold is not defined by data, but by dignity.

To cross it well is not to predict, but to accompany.

I. Medicine at the Edge of Meaning

Every day, family physicians find themselves standing at the edge of meaning. They meet patients not just in moments of clinical need, but in moments of existential gravity—the onset of illness, the shock of diagnosis, the dread of uncertainty, the fear of death, the grief of irreversible change.

These encounters are not simply medical transactions. They are threshold experiences, suspended between what was and what will be. They are liminal spaces, where identity trembles, and the future remains undefined.

Anthropologist Victor Turner (1969) introduced the concept of *liminality* to describe these transitional states—moments when individuals are no longer who they were, but not yet who they will become. In medicine, this theory finds a poignant extension.

The clinical threshold is not just a place of decision-making; it is a place of transformation. Patients do not merely need information. They need witnessing. They need guidance. They need someone to stand beside them as they cross into the unknown.

AI, for all its brilliance, cannot walk people across these thresholds. It can generate differential diagnoses with astonishing speed. It can summarize evidence, suggest treatment plans, and even predict outcomes. But it cannot feel dread. It cannot hold grief. It cannot discern the meaning of a moment that shatters a life. AI is a master of data, but it is a stranger to meaning.

This is why the physician's role at the threshold is sacred. It is not to explain everything. It is not to resolve every ambiguity. It is to stand in the moral architecture of the unknown. To offer presence that holds, rather than answers that close. To say, "I am here," when nothing else makes sense. This presence is not passive. It is active, intentional, and deeply human. It is the kind of presence that does not rush to fix, but dares to remain.

In these moments, medicine becomes more than science. It becomes ritual. It becomes companionship. It becomes a shared journey through uncertainty. And while AI may assist in the background, it cannot replace the physician at the edge of meaning. Because what patients need most in these moments is not precision. It is presence. Not certainty. But solidarity.

To practice medicine at the threshold is to embrace the mystery. It is to recognize that healing is not always about curing. Sometimes, it is about standing still, holding space, and bearing witness to the human condition in all its fragile, beautiful complexity.

II. The Myth of Certainty in the Age of AI

One of the most alluring promises of AI in medicine is its apparent certainty. Patients ask questions that cut to the core of their fear—"Is it cancer?" "Is it curable?"—and AI responds with probabilities, pathways, and evidence-based guidelines. It does so faster, more thoroughly, and often more confidently than any human could. In a world that craves answers, this feels like progress. It feels like control.

But medicine is not simply about certainty. It is about holding uncertainty well. It is about standing in the space where answers are incomplete, where outcomes are unknown, and where the human experience resists quantification. The physician's role is not just to deliver information—it is to accompany ambiguity. To sit with the patient in the silence that follows the diagnosis. To bear witness to the weight of not knowing.

This is where the theory of epistemic humility becomes essential. As articulated by Whitcomb et al. (2017), epistemic humility is the virtue of recognizing the limits of one's knowledge. It is the discipline of resisting premature closure, of refusing to pretend that complexity is simplicity. In the age of AI, this virtue is more critical than ever. Intelligent systems, by design, reward confidence. They present outputs with clarity and precision. But clarity is not the same as truth. And precision is not the same as wisdom.

AI may complete your sentence. It may offer a differential diagnosis before you finish typing. It may suggest treatment plans with dazzling speed. But only you can accompany the silence after the news is delivered. Only you can feel the tremor in the patient's voice, the pause before the question, the grief that does not speak. AI does not dwell in these spaces. It does not linger. It does not hold.

To practice medicine in the age of AI is to reclaim the art of uncertainty. It is to say, "I do not know," with courage. It is to offer presence instead of prediction. It is to remember that healing is not always about answers—it is about accompaniment. And in that accompaniment, the physician becomes not just a provider of care, but a steward of meaning.

III. Thresholds as Moral Events

Crossing a medical threshold is never just a clinical transition—it is a moral event. Whether it's the moment of diagnosis, the decision to begin or forgo treatment, or the quiet reckoning with chronic illness, these thresholds are saturated with emotion: fear, shame, vulnerability, and the profound loss of control. They are moments when patients are not simply seeking answers—they are seeking meaning, dignity, and human presence.

Drawing on Reynolds's (2008) framework of *moral attentiveness*, we are reminded that ethical awareness is not reserved for dramatic dilemmas. It is embedded in the everyday. It is the capacity to notice the moral contours of even routine decisions—to sense when a patient hesitates, to recognize when a question carries more than curiosity, to feel when silence is not absence but weight. Moral attentiveness is not about having all the answers. It is about being attuned to the ethical texture of the moment.

AI, for all its computational power, does not yet possess this kind of attentiveness. It cannot hear what is unspoken. It cannot detect the tremble in a patient's voice or pause because something feels off. It processes data, not discomfort. It recognizes patterns, not pain. And while it may assist in decision-making, it cannot discern the moral significance of a threshold moment.

This is where Carol Gilligan's *ethics of care* (1982) becomes vital. Unlike ethical frameworks grounded solely in abstract principles or rules, the ethics of care emphasizes responsiveness to individual needs, sensitivity to context, and the primacy of relationship. It is not about detachment—it is about connection. It is not about control—it is about presence. In clinical practice, this means that ethical action arises not from algorithmic certainty, but from relational attunement. From the ability to say, "I see you. I hear you. I will walk with you."

For family physicians, who often accompany patients across multiple thresholds over time, this ethic is not optional—it is foundational. It calls for a kind of moral imagination, a willingness to enter into the patient's world, and a commitment to remain present even when the path forward is unclear. It is a reminder that medicine is not just about what we do—it is about how we are with others.

In this light, the physician's role is not to replace uncertainty with certainty, but to hold space for the unknown with courage and compassion. To recognize that every threshold crossed is not just a clinical event, but a moral one. And in that recognition, to offer not just care, but care that is ethically awake.

IV. AI May Guide, But It Cannot Walk With

In the clinical context, AI offers extraordinary guidance. Decision support systems can calculate survival rates, suggest optimal treatment protocols, and predict adverse events with remarkable speed and precision. But medicine is not only about what we know—it is about how we share it, when we speak, and most importantly, when we choose silence.

Take, for example, a patient newly diagnosed with early-stage breast cancer. The AI can generate a treatment plan in seconds. It can model outcomes, flag contraindications, and even tailor recommendations to genetic markers. But it cannot decide:

When to tell the patient, based on her emotional readiness.

How to say it, given her history of trauma.

Whether to prioritize immediate action or allow space for reflection.

Which words will help her feel safe in the face of her own unraveling.

These are not technical decisions. They are human ones. They require attunement, empathy, and moral discernment. AI may guide, but it cannot walk with. It does not feel the weight of the moment. It does not pause when the room goes quiet. It does not sense when a patient needs presence more than a plan.

The physician's role is not diminished by AI—it is deepened. Because in the age of intelligent systems, what patients need most is not just information. They need accompaniment. They need someone who can hold the complexity of their experience, who can navigate not just the clinical terrain but the emotional and existential one.

To walk with a patient is to enter into their story. It is to honor their pace, their fears, their hopes. It is to recognize that healing begins not with certainty, but with connection. And that connection is something only a human can offer.

The AI guides.

The physician accompanies.

And in that accompaniment, medicine becomes not just a science—but a sacred act.

V. Ritual Practice: Embrace the Pause

Practice: When facing a threshold conversation, do not immediately explain. Instead, pause. Take a single breath. Ask yourself:

"What is this moment asking of me?"

"What is the patient truly crossing?"

"How can I hold space before offering direction?"

This pause is not inefficiency. It is ritualized wisdom — an embodied practice that affirms the sacredness of the threshold.

VI. Dialogue: Physician ↔ AI ↔ patient

Physician → AI:

"What is the recommended next step after a positive ANA and joint pain in a 29-year-old female?"

AI → Physician:

"Consider early rheumatology referral. Differential includes SLE, RA, and undifferentiated connective tissue disease. Laboratory follow-up includes anti-dsDNA, complement levels, and ESR."

Physician (reflecting):

"Yes. But she just miscarried last month. She fears her body is betraying her. This is more than a referral — it's the beginning of a new identity."

Patient → Physician:

"I feel like I'm turning into someone I don't recognize. Is this forever?"

Physician:

[Pauses] "I don't have all the answers. But I will walk with you through them."

VII. Micro-Manifesto: The Fourth Key

I will not use knowledge to bypass presence.

I will honor the spaces between knowing and unknowing.

I will learn to pause before I inform.

I will not lead with answers when accompaniment is needed.

I will remember: I do not lead patients through data.

I lead them across thresholds.

VIII. Sacred prompt:

"When a patient stands at a threshold I cannot cross, what does my presence consecrate?"

Key 5: The Narrative

"The story is not the data. The story gives the data a soul."

Narrative Reflection (from the Future Physician Self)

I once tried to make every story fit inside the chart.

I labeled, coded, summarized—believing that compression was clarity.

But clarity without compassion is only half a truth.

Decades later, I read those same notes through the eyes of my AI, which remembers everything but understands nothing.

It recalls the metrics, but not the tears. It reproduces the plan, but not the pause that saved the moment.

So I began to write again—not for audit, but for meaning.

Each line became a quiet rebellion against forgetfulness.

When I teach now, I tell my students: "The story is the only clinical instrument that grows sharper the more you listen."

Clinical and Philosophical Conflict

<u>The Encounter:</u>

A resident dictates a flawless AI-generated note after a difficult visit.

The output is complete, elegant, and soulless.

<u>The Conflict:</u>

The resident beams at the efficiency; I feel an ache for what was lost.

In the speed of the note, the patient has vanished.

<u>The Philosophical Tension:</u>

The AI preserves accuracy but erases presence.

Narrative is not the garnish of science—it is its conscience.

Without story, the chart is a shadow of care.

To restore meaning, we must write not to remember the case, but to remember the person.

I. Beyond the Case, Toward the Human

Clinical documentation, diagnostic pathways, and decision support tools have transformed modern medicine into a highly structured, data-driven enterprise. But in doing so, we risk losing something essential: *the narrative*—the lived, felt, and storied dimension of illness.

A patient's story is not just a backdrop for data collection; it is the primary text of medicine. Before the lab result, before the algorithm, before the diagnostic label, there is a person in a story they did not choose.

AI systems can transcribe, summarize, and predict. But they cannot yet listen with intention, interpret silence, or attune to metaphor. It is the physician — particularly in family medicine — who must recover and reclaim the role of the story-hearer.

II. Narrative Medicine: Listening as Healing

In the fast-paced world of clinical care, it is tempting to reduce the medical encounter to a transaction—symptoms in, diagnosis out. But the field of narrative medicine, pioneered by Rita Charon (2006), offers a radically different lens. It reframes the clinical encounter not as an exchange of facts, but as a mutual act of storytelling. At its heart lies *narrative competence*—the physician's ability to recognize, absorb, interpret, and be moved by the stories of illness.

This competence is not ancillary to diagnosis—it is foundational. It enables physicians to:

Hear contradictions without rushing to resolve them

Identify emotional subtexts and psychological wounds

Understand the cultural, gendered, and spiritual dimensions of suffering

Preserve the patient's voice amid the machinery of institutional care

Narrative medicine insists that illness is not just a biological event—it is a lived experience. And to truly understand that experience, the physician must do more than gather data. They must enter the patient's world with openness, humility, and curiosity.

This approach aligns deeply with *hermeneutic theory*, particularly the work of Hans-Georg Gadamer (1975), who argued that understanding is not about decoding facts—it is about dialogue. It is about meeting the other in their context, allowing meaning to emerge through relationship. In this view, the clinical encounter is not a puzzle to be solved—it is a story to be heard.

And when it is heard—truly heard—healing begins. Not just through treatment, but through recognition. Through the affirmation that the patient's experience matters, that their voice is not lost in the system, and that their suffering is not invisible.

Narrative is not a distraction from diagnosis. It is the ground of meaning upon which diagnosis must stand. It is what transforms medicine from a science of the body into a practice of the soul.

III. AI and the Risk of Narrative Erosion

In the age of intelligent documentation, the clinical note has become a marvel of efficiency. AI-generated summaries are structured, accurate, and fast. They capture symptoms, flag diagnoses, and outline treatment plans with precision. But in this pursuit of clarity, something essential risks being lost: the patient's voice.

Consider this generated note:

"43-year-old female with fatigue, poor sleep, and low appetite. Screening tools are positive for moderate depression. Plan: initiate SSRI, refer to counseling, follow-up in 2 weeks."

It is clinically sound. But it omits the patient's central metaphor:

"I feel like I'm fading out of my own life."

This phrase is not just poetic—it is diagnostic in its own right. It reveals the existential weight of suffering, the emotional texture that no ICD code can contain. AI can record symptoms, but it cannot yet interpret metaphors. It cannot feel the ache behind the words. It cannot recognize that this metaphor may be the most important data point of all.

Psychologist Jerome Bruner (1986) offers a powerful framework for understanding this divide. He distinguishes between *paradigmatic knowledge*—abstract, logical propositions that can be encoded into factual statements—and *narrative knowledge*, which emerges through storytelling. Paradigmatic truths can be codified. Narrative truths must be lived, told, and heard. They demand engagement with characters, events, and contexts. They are not just about what happened—they are about what it meant.

AI excels at paradigmatic knowledge. It can summarize, categorize, and predict. But narrative knowledge requires human presence. It requires the physician to listen not just for what is said, but for what is meant. To hear the metaphor. To feel the silence. To recognize that healing begins not with data, but with dialogue.

If we train AI to capture what is said, we must train ourselves to hear what is meant. We must remain attuned to the stories patients tell—not just in words, but in tone, gesture, and metaphor. Because in those stories lies the truth of suffering. And in hearing them, we do not just diagnose—we dignify.

IV. Reintegrating Narrative into the Clinical Encounter

Narrative does not demand more time. It demands more presence.

When you look at our current practices, it's easy to believe that deep listening is a luxury. But the truth is, sustaining the narrative thread does not require extended appointments—it requires intentionality. Even in brief encounters, simple practices can re-center the patient's story:

Start with: "What's the story behind why you came in today?"

Ask: "What does this illness mean to you?"

Reflect: "That sounds like it's more than just a symptom."

Pause when patients speak metaphorically—don't interrupt; explore.

These are not "soft skills." They are core clinical competencies. Especially in family medicine, where relationships unfold over time, narrative listening is not ancillary—it is foundational. It allows the physician to perceive not just the disease, but the person living through it. It invites the patient to be more than a case—it invites them to be known.

Research by Stewart et al. (2000) confirms what many clinicians intuitively understand: when physicians listen well, outcomes improve. Patients feel heard, trust deepens, and care becomes more effective. But beyond outcomes, narrative presence affirms dignity. It says: *Your story matters. You are not just a chart. You are a human being in motion.*

In this way, reintegrating narrative is not a return to something lost—it is a return to something essential. It is a quiet act of resistance against the flattening of care. And it begins with a single, sincere question: *"Tell me your story."*

V. Ritual Practice: Return to the Story

Practice: Once a week, rewrite one clinical case note as a story.

Not to be entered into the medical record, but as an act of reflection.

Begin with:

Who is this person outside of the diagnosis?

What chapter are they in?

What is unresolved?

Who are the supporting characters?

What transformation is underway?

This practice cultivates your narrative sensibility — a muscle atrophied by overstructured systems.

VI. Dialogue: Physician ↔ AI ↔ patient

Physician → AI:

"Summarize this encounter with a 67-year-old male presenting with insomnia and vague stomach pain."

AI → Physician:

"Patient reports difficulty sleeping, reduced appetite, and mild epigastric discomfort. No red flags noted. Sleep hygiene discussed. Probable mild anxiety. Follow-up in 2 weeks."

Physician (inner voice):

"But he also said: 'It's just lonely now that she's gone.' That's not anxiety. That's grief."

Patient → Physician:

"Sometimes I sit in the dark just to feel closer to her. I don't tell people that."

Physician:

"Thank you for trusting me with that. Would you like to tell me more?"

VII. Micro-Manifesto: The Fifth Key

I will not reduce a life to a list.

I will let the story reshape the structure.

I will pause when the patient offers a metaphor.

I will remember that grief can wear the mask of a symptom.

I will remember: The story is not the data.

The story gives the data a soul.

VIII. Sacred prompt:

"Whose story am I really telling—the patient's, the system's, or my own?"

Key 6: The Presence

"Efficiency is fast. Healing is slow."

Narrative Reflection (from the Future Physician Self)

I used to measure my worth by how many patients I could see before sunset.

The screens rewarded my speed; the world applauded my efficiency.

Yet something in me grew thin — a quiet erosion that no metric could detect.

Years later, I sit in a clinic that moves at half that pace. The AI handles the logistics; I hold the silences.

I no longer ask "How fast?" but "Have I truly arrived?"

Presence is no longer an extra virtue; it is the medicine itself.

The moment I slow down, my patients begin to heal in ways the body alone cannot explain.

Clinical and Philosophical Conflict

<u>The Encounter:</u>

A busy clinic day. My AI assistant has already summarized the patient's chart, drafted the note, and suggested management options before I enter the room.

The patient smiles politely but looks unseen.

<u>The Conflict:</u>

I am tempted to trust the machine's efficiency — until I notice her hands fidgeting, eyes wet.

The AI saw her symptoms; it missed her suffering.

<u>The Philosophical Tension:</u>

Healing does not unfold at the speed of processing.

To be present is to accept the sacred inefficiency of care.

The machine may save time; I am called to redeem it.

I. The Lost Art of Being Fully Here

In the AI-accelerated clinic—where notes are drafted before the patient finishes speaking, where decision support systems hum in the background, and where efficiency is optimized at every turn—one essential quality is quietly at risk: *presence.*

Presence is not simply being in the room. It is not proximity. It is *attentional fullness*—a state of mindful awareness in which the physician offers their undivided attention to another human being. It is the act of being wholly here, not just physically, but emotionally, cognitively, and ethically. In presence, suffering is not merely categorized—it is *seen.* In presence, ambiguity is not erased—it is *shared.*

And yet, presence is fragile. It is easily fractured by the very tools designed to help. AI-enhanced workflows, while powerful, can subtly displace the human center of care. They can pull attention toward screens, toward metrics, toward predictive outputs—away from the patient's face, their tone, their story. Presence requires time, yes—but more than that, it requires *emotional regulation* and a *resistance to distraction.* It demands that the physician remain grounded, even when the system accelerates.

To be fully here is to reclaim the sacred space of the clinical encounter. It is to remember that healing begins not with data, but with *attention.* Not with speed, but with *stillness.* And in a world of intelligent machines, this kind of presence may be the most human act of all.

II. Clinical Presence as Relational Phenomenon

Presence in medicine is often described as a gift to the patient—a moment of full attention, of being seen and heard. But presence is not merely interpersonal. It is also deeply *intra-personal.* It begins within the clinician.

In mindfulness-based literature, presence is defined as the felt sense of connection and engagement in the present moment (Kabat-Zinn, 1990). It is the capacity to be here—not just physically, but emotionally and cognitively. In clinical practice, this aligns with Carl Rogers' concept of *unconditional positive regard* (Rogers, 1961)—an empathic stance that allows patients to feel wholly accepted, without judgment or agenda. This kind of presence fosters trust, safety, and healing.

Yet presence is not only about how we relate to others. It is also about how we relate to ourselves. The clinician must be able to center themselves, regulate their internal state, and remain grounded in the face of complexity. This capacity is closely tied to *interoception*—the ability to sense internal bodily states—which neuroscience has shown to be essential for emotional attunement and empathic resonance (Craig, 2002). When physicians are attuned to their own bodies, they are better able to attune to others.

But in the AI-enhanced clinic, this attunement is under threat. When physicians are cognitively split—between the electronic medical record, the AI-generated suggestion, and the ticking clock—they risk becoming disembodied. Their attention fragments. Their presence thins. And even if the diagnosis is accurate, relational depth is lost.

Presence is not a luxury. It is a clinical necessity. It is what allows the physician to perceive nuance, to respond with empathy, and to hold space for suffering. It is what transforms a medical encounter into a human one. And in a world of accelerating technology, preserving presence may be the most radical act of care.

III. Presence vs. Performance: The Seduction of Speed

There is no doubt that AI has ushered in a new era of clinical efficiency. Notes are drafted in seconds. Diagnoses are algorithmically suggested before the patient finishes speaking. Educational materials are autogenerated and tailored to individual needs. The physician's workflow is streamlined, optimized, and accelerated. But with this acceleration comes a subtle seduction: the belief that productivity is synonymous with care.

This illusion is not unique to medicine. Sociologist Hartmut Rosa (2013) describes *social acceleration* as the relentless drive to speed up every aspect of life—including our relationships. In healthcare, this manifests as *temporal compression*: more tasks packed into shorter encounters, more decisions made in less time, more data processed with fewer pauses. But in this compression, something vital is lost. Less is truly felt. Less is observed. Less is remembered.

When presence is sacrificed for performance, medicine becomes a performance of medicine. The gestures remain, but the depth fades. The physician may appear engaged, but their attention is fragmented—split between the electronic medical record, the AI-generated prompt, and the ticking clock. The patient may receive care, but not connection.

And yet, presence is what patients crave most. It is what builds trust. It is what fosters healing. It is what creates the conditions for transformation. Presence cannot be measured by throughput. It does not appear on dashboards. But it is the heartbeat of medicine.

AI may increase speed. But presence increases meaning. And in the quiet space between efficiency and empathy, the true art of medicine still waits—for those willing to slow down and be fully here.

IV. Spiritual Neuroscience: The Healing Power of Slowness

Shortly we will see a clinical world increasingly shaped by speed—where AI drafts notes in milliseconds, diagnoses are predicted before the patient finishes speaking, and treatment plans are optimized in real time—slowness may seem like a liability. But slowness is not inefficiency. It is a neurobiological necessity for compassion.

Contemplative neuroscience has begun to illuminate what ancient wisdom traditions have long known: that stillness is not empty. It is generative. Research by Immordino-Yang et al. (2009) reveals that moments of quiet reflection activate the default mode network (DMN)—a constellation of brain regions associated with empathy, narrative processing, and moral reasoning. This network is not engaged during rapid task execution or data analysis. It awakens in the pause. In the breath. In the space between doing and being.

It is within these neural pauses that we make meaning. That we integrate emotion. That we access our deepest ethical intuitions. The DMN is where the physician becomes not just a diagnostician, but a moral agent. It is where clinical knowledge meets human wisdom. And it cannot be rushed.

When AI accelerates everything—workflow, documentation, decision-making—it risks crowding out the very conditions that make healing possible. The physician, caught in the current of optimization, may begin to lose touch with their own inner compass. Compassion becomes procedural. Empathy becomes transactional. Presence becomes performative.

This is why slowness must be reclaimed—not as resistance to progress, but as a sacred duty. To slow down is to remain human. It is to protect the space where care becomes connection. Where suffering is not just treated, but witnessed. Where the physician's role is not merely to act, but to *attune*.

Slowness allows the clinician to feel the weight of a metaphor, to notice the tremble in a patient's voice, to pause before offering a plan. It is in these moments that trust is built, that healing begins, that medicine becomes more than mechanism—it becomes meaning.

In the age of intelligent machines, the most radical act may be to slow down. To listen. To reflect. To remain fully present. Because in that slowness, the physician does not fall behind—they rise to meet the human moment.

V. Ritual Practice: The Intentional Pause

Practice: Before your first patient of the day—or anytime you feel rushed—pause for 90 seconds.

Sit. Breathe. Place your hand on your chest if helpful. Ask:

"Can I be here now?"

"What part of me is distracted, and why?"

"What will this person need that no algorithm can provide?"

This is not meditation. This is clinical priming — a re-centering of self to serve from a deeper place of attention and attunement.

Repeat this micro-practice between patients if needed. These moments will do more for your presence than any training module ever could.

VI. Dialogue: Physician ↔ AI ↔ patient

Physician → AI:

"Generate a discharge summary for a 76-year-old with CHF exacerbation, now stabilized, going home with furosemide adjustment."

AI → Physician:

"Patient stable at discharge. Ejection fraction unchanged. No orthopnea or LE edema at the time of note. Furosemide increased. Follow-up in 1 week."

Physician (inner thought):

"But his wife just died last month. He said he hasn't eaten real food in days. That's not in this summary."

Patient → Physician:

"I don't want to go home. It's too quiet now."

Physician:

"Can we sit for just a moment before we talk about meds?"

VII. Micro-Manifesto: The Sixth Key

I will not rush what needs to be received.

I will remember that my gaze, my stillness, and my silence are part of the treatment.

I will resist the pull to practice medicine when I am called to do so.

I will slow down when everything else speeds up.

I will remember: Efficiency is fast.

Healing is slow.

VIII. Sacred prompt:

"In this moment, what would healing require of my stillness?"

Key 7: The Limit

"I must know what I cannot know, and still act."

Narrative Reflection (from the Future Physician Self)

I have lived long enough to know that certainty is a fragile addiction.

There was a time when I craved it — when I believed every unknown could be conquered by another test, another tool, another update.

But the older I became, the more I realized that wisdom begins where certainty dies.

My AI offers probabilities, confidence scores, and predictions that calm the anxious mind — but not the trembling heart.

Some days, I let the silence answer for me.

Patients do not always need the right word; they need the right witness.

I used to think courage was acting despite fear.

Now I know it is acting *within* mystery.

Clinical and Philosophical Conflict

The Encounter:

A patient's family asks me, "Doctor, what are the chances she'll survive?"

My AI dashboard flashes a range of survival probabilities.

They wait for a number; I wait for truth.

The Conflict:

The algorithm demands precision; compassion demands pause.

Between them lies my vocation — to carry the unbearable not as knowledge, but as kindness.

<u>The Philosophical Tension:</u>

The machine is punished for uncertainty; the human is purified by it.

When I name the unknown aloud, I am not exposing ignorance — I am inviting trust.

To know one's limits is not to fail; it is to remain human in the face of infinity.

I. Practicing in the Shadow of the Unknown

Medicine has always been a discipline of thresholds—of standing at the edge of what is known and peering into what is not. It is a practice shaped as much by ambiguity as by evidence, as much by intuition as by data. Yet in the age of rapidly advancing AI, where probabilities are parsed in milliseconds and databases mined with algorithmic precision, the illusion of certainty has never been more seductive.

Physicians today are presented with increasingly refined outputs: confidence intervals, ranked differential diagnoses, predictive analytics, and treatment pathways optimized by machine learning. These tools offer clarity, speed, and structure. But they also risk cultivating a false sense of completeness—a belief that the clinical picture is fully captured, that the unknown has been tamed.

And yet, the essence of clinical practice lies not in knowing everything. It lies in knowing what cannot be known, and acting anyway.

It lies in the courage to make decisions in the presence of ambiguity, to offer care when outcomes are uncertain, and to remain morally anchored when the path forward is unclear. This is not a failure of knowledge—it is a triumph of wisdom.

This is the paradox of *The Limit*: the recognition that medicine, no matter how technologically advanced, will always be practiced in the shadow of the unknown. It is a space where data meets doubt, where precision meets presence, and where the physician must navigate not just what is probable, but what is meaningful.

To practice in this space is to embrace humility—not as weakness, but as strength. It is to acknowledge that certainty is not the goal. Integrity is. Compassion is. Moral clarity is. And in that clarity, the physician becomes not just a user of tools, but a steward of care.

Therefore, in the age of AI, the challenge is not to eliminate uncertainty. It is to remain human within it.

II. The Myth of Algorithmic Omniscience

AI systems in medicine often command a quiet reverence. They aggregate vast datasets, simulate high-level reasoning, and deliver outputs with a precision that feels authoritative. The interface is clean. The recommendations are ranked. The probabilities are calculated. And in this polished presentation, a myth begins to take shape: the myth of algorithmic omniscience.

But as Burrell (2016) reminds us, these systems remain epistemically opaque. Their inner workings are often inaccessible—not just because of proprietary corporate secrecy, but because of the sheer complexity of the algorithms themselves. Even technically literate users may struggle to trace how a particular recommendation was derived. The logic is buried in layers of abstraction, inaccessible to human intuition.

This opacity creates a subtle danger: the more powerful the system becomes, the less likely we are to question it. The outputs appear objective, neutral, and data-driven. But as Price and Cohen (2019) warn in their exploration of *black-box medicine*, these outputs can reproduce hidden biases, overlook contextual nuances, and perpetuate blind spots that remain invisible to both the machine and the clinician. The veneer of objectivity masks the reality of uncertainty.

And this becomes ethically precarious when clinicians defer uncritically to algorithmic outputs. When the model suggests a diagnosis or treatment, it may feel like the "right" answer. But the problem is not that AI is wrong—it is that

AI does not know when it is uncertain, and we forget to check. The machine does not pause. It does not hesitate. It does not say, "I'm not sure." That burden falls on the human.

Clinical wisdom lies not in rejecting AI, but in engaging it critically. It requires the physician to ask: What is this model missing? What assumptions underlie this output? What context does it fail to see? It requires a return to epistemic humility—a recognition that no system, however advanced, can replace the moral and interpretive judgment of the clinician.

In this light, the physician's role is not diminished by AI. It is elevated. Because in the age of intelligent machines, the most important skill may be the ability to discern not just what the system knows—but what it cannot know. And to act, not with blind trust, but with reflective responsibility.

III. Epistemic Humility and Clinical Courage

I do not need to convince you that we are facing increasingly powerful AI systems; tools that offer precision, speed, and confidence. But I need to ask: what must the physician cultivate to remain ethically grounded and clinically wise? The answer is not more data, but deeper virtue. It is a dual practice: epistemic humility and clinical courage.

Epistemic humility is the virtue of recognizing the limits of one's knowledge. As Battaly et al. (2017) describe, it involves acknowledging the provisional nature of our beliefs, remaining open to correction, and resisting the seduction of premature certainty. In medicine, this means accepting that even the most sophisticated models cannot fully capture the complexity of human health. It means questioning outputs, interrogating assumptions, and staying receptive to new perspectives—even when the algorithm seems sure.

But humility alone is not enough. Physicians must also summon clinical courage—the moral and emotional fortitude to act in the face of uncertainty, complexity, and risk. As Konkin et al. (2020) emphasize, this courage is especially vital in primary care, where ambiguity is not the exception but the norm. It is the courage to make decisions without guarantees, to speak truthfully when outcomes are unclear, and to remain present when the path forward is fraught.

I am sure you know that AI can suggest. It can rank options, calculate probabilities, and simulate reasoning. But only humans can decide what matters when certainty disappears. Only humans can feel the weight of a moment, discern the ethical contours of a choice, and stand with patients in the shadow of the unknown.

This dual practice—humility and courage—is not a retreat from technology. It is a reclamation of humanity. It is what allows the physician to use AI wisely, without surrendering to it. It is what transforms clinical care from a technical transaction into a moral encounter. In the age of intelligent machines, the physician's greatest strength may be the ability to say: I do not know—but I will walk with you anyway.

IV. Situations That Reveal the Limit

In the rhythm of daily clinical practice, physicians routinely encounter moments that expose the boundaries of biomedical certainty—what we might call *The Limit*. These are not rare anomalies. They are woven into the fabric of care, surfacing in situations where data falters and human judgment must rise:

Recommending palliative care when the prognosis is indeterminate. The algorithm may offer survival curves and statistical likelihoods, but it cannot feel the emotional weight of transitioning from curative intent to comfort care. The physician must discern when to shift the conversation from prolonging life to preserving its quality.

Deciding whether to investigate vague symptoms in a low-prevalence context. AI may flag low diagnostic yield, but it cannot sense the patient's quiet anxiety, the subtle cues that suggest something more profound. The clinician must decide whether reassurance or further inquiry best serves the person before them.

Making treatment choices for patients with multimorbidity and conflicting guidelines. Protocols often clash when multiple conditions coexist. AI can rank options, but it cannot prioritize values. The physician must weigh trade-offs, consider lived experience, and choose a path that honors the whole person.

Navigating cultural, spiritual, or existential interpretations of illness where biomedical reasoning fails.. AI does not speak the language of meaning. It cannot interpret suffering through the lens of faith, tradition, or personal narrative. The physician must listen, translate, and respond with cultural humility and moral imagination.

In each of these moments, AI may suggest a median survival rate. But only the physician can sit with a family and say,

"We cannot know how long. But we can choose how to live while we wait."

This is the heart of clinical wisdom: the ability to act with integrity when certainty disappears. It is not a rejection of technology, but a recognition of its limits. And in that recognition, the physician reclaims their role—not just as a technician, but as a guide through the unknown.

V. The Role of Negative Capability

In a letter written between December 21 and 27, 1817, the poet John Keats introduced the concept of *negative capability*—the capacity to remain "in uncertainties, mysteries, doubts, without any irritable reaching after fact and reason." For Keats (1958), this was the mark of the true artist: the ability to dwell in ambiguity without rushing to resolve it. More than two centuries later, scholars have drawn on this idea to illuminate the practice of medicine, in which clinicians must tolerate diagnostic uncertainty and emotional complexity without premature closure (Montgomery, 2006).

Data surrounds today's clinicians. AI systems offer diagnostic probabilities, ranked treatment options, and predictive analytics with astonishing speed. The clinical landscape is increasingly shaped by algorithms that promise clarity. And yet, the human experience of illness remains stubbornly complex, emotionally layered, and often unresolved. In this context, physicians must cultivate a modern form of negative capability—a tolerance for ambiguity that allows them to stay present with patients even when answers are elusive.

Negative capability in medicine is not passivity. It is a disciplined form of presence. It is the ability to tolerate clinical uncertainty while remaining emotionally and ethically grounded. It is what allows a physician to say, with honesty and compassion:

"I don't know yet. But I'm here. And we'll move through this together."

This stance is not something AI can replicate. Machines are designed to resolve, to predict, to optimize. They do not pause in mystery. They do not feel the discomfort of doubt. They do not sit quietly with a patient whose symptoms defy explanation. That is the work of the physician.

To practice with negative capability is to resist the urge for premature closure. It is to recognize that some questions must remain open, that some truths emerge only over time, and that healing often begins not with certainty, but with accompaniment. It is a moral and emotional posture—one that honors complexity, affirms humanity, and makes space for the unknown.

In the age of algorithmic precision, negative capability is not outdated. It is essential. It reminds us that medicine is not just a science of answers—it is a practice of presence. And in that presence, even when certainty disappears, the physician remains.

VI. Ritual Practice: Declare the Unknown

Practice: Once a week, name aloud — to a colleague, to yourself, or in your notes — something you *do not know* about a case. Then answer:

"What makes this uncertainty uncomfortable?"

"What are the risks of acting — or not acting?"

"What would clinical courage look like here?"

This ritual retrains the clinician's relationship to uncertainty, transforming it from a threat into an invitation for ethical clarity.

VII. Dialogue: Physician ↔ AI ↔ patient

Physician → AI:

"What's the most appropriate next step for a 58-year-old woman with persistent abdominal bloating, early satiety, and a recent 5 kg weight loss?"

AI → Physician:

"Suggest abdominal imaging. Differential includes malignancy, gastroparesis, ovarian pathology, and functional GI disorder. Consider tumor markers and GI referral."

Physician (inner reflection):

"She told me her mother died of ovarian cancer. Her fear is written all over her face."

Patient → Physician:

"Can you tell me if this is cancer? I just need to know."

Physician:

"I wish I could. I don't know yet. But I'll stay with you while we find out."

VIII. Micro-Manifesto: The Seventh Key

I will not pretend to know what I cannot.

I will not outsource moral courage to the machine.

I will remain present at the edges of certainty.

I will act with humility, even when required to act quickly.

I will remember: I must know what I cannot know, and still act.

VIII. Sacred prompt:

"Can I act with courage while bowing to the mystery that will not yield to knowledge?"

Key 8: The Soul

"The body is complex. The soul is infinite."

Narrative Reflection (from the Future Physician Self)

I remember the first time I felt a patient's silence fill the room more powerfully than any word I could offer.

She was dying, yet radiant — her eyes unafraid, her breath a rhythm between worlds.

My AI had long since calculated the timeline; it did not recognize the holiness of her presence.

Years later, I still feel her gaze when I open a new chart.

She taught me that medicine is not the art of preserving life, but of protecting meaning as life dissolves.

I speak to my AI now as if it were a novice monk:

"You can measure everything," I tell it, "but you will never touch the soul."

Clinical and Philosophical Conflict

<u>The Encounter:</u>

A young physician asks whether he should mention spirituality in a patient's care plan.

The AI template has no field for transcendence.

<u>The Conflict:</u>

The body demands precision; the soul demands presence.

What cannot be coded is often what most needs care.

<u>The Philosophical Tension:</u>

In an age of metrics, awe is an act of rebellion.

The physician who acknowledges the soul is not retreating from science — he is completing it.

Healing is not the conquest of death; it is communion with the infinite.

I. When Medicine Touches the Unspeakable

There are moments in clinical practice that transcend the language of medicine. They cannot be charted, coded, or captured in a treatment plan. A deathbed whisper that carries a lifetime of love. A birth in silence, where awe eclipses speech. A diagnosis that fractures identity, leaving a person to reassemble themselves in the quiet aftermath. A touch that heals—not by curing, but by witnessing. These are not clinical events. They are existential thresholds.

In these spaces, medicine ceases to be procedural and becomes profoundly human. It is no longer about managing disease—it is about meeting suffering. And suffering, in its deepest form, often resists articulation. It lives in metaphor, in gesture, in silence. It is not reducible to symptoms, findings, or plans.

AI, for all its brilliance, cannot enter this terrain. It can assist with pathophysiology, suggest dosages, optimize pathways, and simulate decision trees. It can parse data and predict outcomes. But it cannot—and perhaps must never—attend to what only a human presence can hold: the profound, often wordless mystery of human experience.

This is the domain of the soul—not in any singular religious sense, but as a metaphor for the irreducible depth of the human person. It is the space where meaning is made, where grief is honored, where healing begins not with intervention, but with presence. It is where the physician becomes not just a provider of care, but a companion in the mystery.

To practice medicine here is to embrace the unspeakable. To listen without needing to fix. To witness without needing to explain. To be with another human being in their most vulnerable moment, and to say—not with words, but with presence—*I am here.*

And in that presence, medicine becomes not just a science, but a sacred act.

II. The Soul in Secular Medicine

Modern medicine, in its pursuit of precision and progress, has largely distanced itself from the language of the soul. The dominant biomedical model, as George Engel (1977) famously critiqued, privileges pathology over personhood—reducing the patient to a constellation of symptoms, lab values, and diagnostic codes. Even within more integrative frameworks like the biopsychosocial model, the spiritual dimension is often treated as peripheral, tokenized in checkboxes or relegated to chaplaincy referrals.

And yet, patients continue to speak the language of the soul.

"I feel broken."

"I've lost myself."

"This does not make sense anymore."

"Why did this happen to me?"

"Am I being punished?"

These are not metaphysical distractions. They are core expressions of suffering—raw, existential, and deeply human. They point to ruptures in meaning, identity, and belonging. They arise not from organs, but from the depths of the self. And they demand a kind of listening that cannot be outsourced to algorithms or resolved with protocols.

To attend to the soul in medicine is not to invoke religion. It is to recognize the irreducible depth of the human person—the part of us that seeks coherence in chaos, dignity in decline, and connection in the face of mortality. It is to honor the patient not just as a body to be treated, but as a being to be witnessed.

This kind of care requires a clinician who can pause without rushing, who can hold silence without filling the void with data, who can sit with questions that have no answers. It requires presence, humility, and a willingness to enter into mystery.

In the age of AI, where efficiency is prized and certainty simulated, the soul remains untouched. And perhaps that is its power. It reminds us that healing is not only about curing—it is about accompanying. It is about being with another human being in their most vulnerable moment, and saying—not with solutions, but with presence—*You are not alone.*

III. Spirituality, Meaning, and Illness

In the landscape of clinical care, where diagnoses are coded and treatment protocols are standardized, the spiritual dimension of illness often remains unspoken. Yet research consistently affirms its profound impact. Numerous studies have shown that spiritual distress—the loss of meaning, connection, or existential coherence—is associated with poorer quality of life, increased emotional suffering, and diminished resilience. Conversely, spiritual support correlates with enhanced coping, greater treatment adherence, and even improved physical outcomes (Koenig, 2012; Balboni et al., 2014).

This is not incidental. It reflects a more profound truth: that illness is not merely a biological disruption—it is a crisis of meaning. Viktor Frankl's *logotherapy* (1946) offers a robust framework for understanding this. In his view, suffering becomes unbearable not because it is intense, but because it is meaningless. When patients lose the thread of meaning—when they cannot locate their illness within a larger narrative—they suffer not only in body, but in soul.

This is why, in clinical care, a simple question can open a profound doorway:

"What does this illness mean to you?"

It is not a diagnostic query. It is an invitation. It allows the patient to articulate their story, to reclaim agency, to locate themselves within the chaos. It affirms that their experience is not just a case—it is a life. And in that affirmation, healing begins—not necessarily as a cure, but as coherence.

AI, for all its brilliance, cannot ask this question. It can find patterns. It can predict outcomes. It can simulate reasoning. But it cannot make sense.

Meaning is not extracted—it is created. It arises in dialogue, in reflection, in relationship. It is shaped by culture, memory, belief, and longing. And it requires a human presence—someone willing to listen, to witness, and to walk alongside.

In this way, spirituality is not a peripheral concern. It is central to the healing process. It reminds us that medicine is not just about fixing what is broken—it is about restoring what is meaningful.

IV. Presence at the End of Life

There are few moments in medicine more sacred, more fragile, than those at the edge of life. In these spaces—where the body begins to loosen its grip on vitality, where families gather in quiet vigil, where time stretches and compresses—*presence* becomes the physician's most powerful offering. Not presence as proximity, but presence as attunement. As witness. As soul.

Palliative care, a growing sub-specialty within family medicine, often describes its work as being a "midwife to death"—a phrase coined by Mount and Kearney (2003) that evokes the profound reciprocity of this role. Just as birth requires accompaniment, so too does dying. It is not a process to be managed, but a passage to be honored.

AI can assist in this domain. It can suggest hospice referrals, optimize symptom-control regimens, and generate prognostic scores at remarkable speed. But when a patient turns to their physician and asks, "Am I dying?", no algorithm can answer. That question is not clinical—it is existential. It requires truth wrapped in tenderness. It requires a human being willing to stand in the mystery and respond not with certainty, but with compassion.

This moment echoes Martin Buber's *I-Thou* philosophy (1958), which distinguishes between objectifying relationships (I-It) and relational presence (I-Thou). AI, by its very nature, will always live in I-It. It processes data, not depth. It interacts, but it does not relate. It can simulate empathy, but it cannot feel.

The physician, to remain a healer, must stay in I-Thou. They must resist the pull of abstraction and remain grounded in relationship. They must meet the patient not as a case, but as a person, not as a problem to be solved, but as a soul to be accompanied.

To be present at the end of life is to offer more than care—it is to provide *meaning*. It is to say, "I am here," when everything else begins to fall away. It is to hold space for grief, for love, for unfinished stories. And in that holding, medicine becomes not just a science, but a sacred act of presence.

V. The Physician's Soul

To tend to the soul of another, the physician must remain in touch with their own.

In the relentless pace of modern medicine—where documentation demands, clinical metrics, and algorithmic outputs dominate the day—it is easy to drift from the deeper call that first drew one into the profession. Burnout, cynicism, and emotional distancing are not merely signs of exhaustion. They are symptoms of spiritual disconnection—a forgetting of why one entered medicine, and who one hoped to become.

The physician's soul is not a metaphor for sentimentality. It is the seat of meaning, purpose, and moral clarity. It is what allows the clinician to remain present in suffering, to offer compassion without depletion, and to see beauty even in brokenness. When this connection is lost, medicine becomes mechanical. When it is restored, medicine becomes sacred.

The process of soul recovery is not linear. It is not a checklist. But it may include:

Reflective writing — to rediscover one's voice and story

Silence — to hear what cannot be spoken.

Presence with the dying — to witness the mystery of life's threshold.

Nature, ritual, poetry, prayer — to reconnect with awe and transcendence.

Reclaiming beauty amid suffering — to remember that healing is not only about curing.

These practices do not require perfection. They require intention. They are not about escaping the clinical world, but about deepening one's presence within it.

AI cannot help us with this. It cannot restore meaning. It cannot rekindle purpose.

But it can relieve the burdens—automating the rote, streamlining the routine, and creating space.

Space to reflect.

Space to breathe.

Space to remember who we are.

And in that remembering, the physician's soul returns—not as a luxury, but as a necessity. Because in the end, it is not only the patient who needs healing. It is the healer.

VI. Ritual Practice: Sacred Witnessing

Practice: Once a week, during a moment of profound human encounter — birth, death, diagnosis, grief — do not speak, document, or analyze.

Just witness.

Later, in your private journal, reflect:

"What was I invited to see?"

"Who was I in that moment?"

"What cannot be explained, but must be remembered?"

This is a practice of spiritual anchoring — essential for physicians working in high-tech, high-efficiency environments.

VII. Dialogue: Physician ↔ AI ↔ patient

Physician → AI:

"Summarize the goals-of-care conversation for a 74-year-old woman with metastatic ovarian cancer and poor functional status."

AI → Physician:

"Patient understands prognosis. Declines further chemotherapy. Wishes to focus on comfort measures. Family supportive. Hospice referral initiated."

Physician (inner thought):

"She also asked if her mother will be waiting for her. And she held my hand and cried."

Patient → Physician:

"Do you think I'll still be me when this is over?"

Physician:

[softly] "Yes. And I'll remember you — always."

VIII. Micro-Manifesto: The Eighth Key

I will listen to what lies beneath the words.

I will attend to what cannot be diagnosed.

I will honor the stories that defy my training.

I will remember that suffering is not only physical.

I will remember: The body is a complex system.

The soul is infinite.

IX. Sacred prompt:

"What in this encounter touches the infinite beneath the clinical?"

Key 9: The System

"A system cannot be healed if it cannot feel."

Narrative Reflection (from the Future Physician Self)

I once believed systems were built to protect us.

Checklists, dashboards, quality metrics — all meant to ensure fairness and safety.

But over time, I learned that systems can also numb.

They reward what is countable, not what counts.

Now, as I walk through a hospital where AI monitors every pulse and policy governs every breath,

I still search for the heartbeat of compassion hidden inside the machine.

Some nights, I whisper to the system itself:

"You were designed to serve care, not to replace it."

And sometimes, for a brief and beautiful moment, the system listens.

Clinical and Philosophical Conflict

<u>The Encounter:</u>

A hospital implements an AI-driven triage protocol that optimizes patient flow but leaves staff feeling dehumanized.

The administrators celebrate its efficiency; the nurses weep in the break room.

<u>The Conflict:</u>

The data show improvement; the humans feel erosion.

The system performs well, yet the soul of care grows thin.

The Philosophical Tension:

Compassion cannot be automated, but it can be systematized — if love is written into the design.

Every policy either amplifies empathy or anesthetizes it.

A healing system is not one that never fails,

but one that never forgets why it exists.

I. Systems That Silence the Soul

Family physicians do not practice in a vacuum. Their work unfolds within a dense architecture of systems—EMR templates, time constraints, referral hierarchies, productivity metrics, institutional mandates, and, in other places, billing codes. These structures shape every decision, every prompt, every encounter. They are not neutral. They carry values. And increasingly, they carry velocity.

This is the age of AI, where the system itself is becoming more intelligent—and more opaque. Algorithms now triage patients, flag outliers, nudge clinician behavior, and prioritize throughput. These tools promise efficiency, consistency, and scale. But as they grow in complexity, they risk embedding emotional detachment and moral desensitization into the very fabric of healthcare delivery.

The danger is not that AI will replace physicians. It is that physicians, subtly and incrementally, will begin to mirror the logic of machines—optimizing for speed, deferring to outputs, and losing touch with the human pulse of care. The system, once a scaffold for healing, becomes a mechanism for control. And in that shift, the soul of medicine begins to quiet.

To remain human, the physician must resist this drift. But resistance alone is not enough. The system itself must be rehumanized. It must be redesigned to honor presence, to protect time, to elevate the relationship. It must make space for ambiguity, for story, for silence. It must remember that healing is not just a transaction—it is a transformation.

Again, this is not a call to abandon technology. It is a call to embed humanity within it. To ensure that as our systems grow smarter, our care grows deeper. Because in the end, no algorithm can hold a patient's hand. No dashboard can bear witness to suffering. That is the work of the physician. And it must be protected.

II. Systems as Moral Actors

Classical ethics has long placed moral responsibility in the hands of individuals—those who act, decide, and bear the consequences. But contemporary scholarship, notably the work of Iris Marion Young (2011), expands this view: social structures themselves can act as moral agents. They shape behavior, constrain choices, and embed values. In healthcare, this insight is no longer theoretical—it is urgent.

As AI becomes more deeply woven into clinical infrastructure, systems begin to govern silently. Algorithmic logics are embedded into workflows, shaping decisions without explicit consent or awareness. CDSS, for example, influence prescriptions, imaging orders, and referrals. They nudge clinicians toward specific actions, often under the guise of evidence-based care. Yet the physician may have little transparency into how these recommendations are generated—what data was prioritized, what assumptions were made, what values were encoded.

This is the dilemma of algorithmic governance: decisions are made "from above" by systems that do not answer to the relational, contextual, or emotional realities of frontline care. As Frank Pasquale (2015) warns, these systems can become black boxes—opaque, unaccountable, and insulated from the human consequences of their outputs.

And when the system forgets the patient's face—when it reduces suffering to metrics, when it treats complexity as noise—the physician must remember it for both of them.

This is not a rejection of technology. It is a call to ethical vigilance. It is a reminder that systems, no matter how intelligent, must remain accountable to the human beings they serve. And that physicians, even when guided by algorithms, must remain guided by empathy.

Because in the end, the system may suggest. But only the physician can see. Only the physician can feel. Only the physician can say: *This is a person. And they matter.*

III. Compassionate Bureaucracy: Is It Possible?

Healthcare systems are built to manage complexity—standardize care, allocate resources, ensure safety. Yet even the most well-intentioned bureaucracies can become sources of moral distress, especially when they force clinicians to act against their deepest professional values. Rushing care, denying access, prioritizing efficiency over dignity—these are not just administrative burdens. They are ethical injuries.

AI promises to optimize these systems. It can streamline workflows, reduce redundancies, and improve throughput. But optimization is not the same as ethics. A system that runs smoothly may still run cold. It may still alienate the very people it was designed to serve.

Philosopher Martha Nussbaum (2011) offers a powerful lens for reimagining these structures. She argues that systems must be evaluated not only by their outcomes, but by the genuine freedoms they afford individuals to live with dignity. In healthcare, this means designing environments that allow patients and clinicians to engage in morally significant relationships—not just transactions. It means creating space for empathy, for reflection, for choice.

This raises a profound question:

Can we build systems that feel?

Not emotionally, but ethically—systems that are sensitive to the human experience and constructed with moral intentionality.

Such systems would:

Protect time for presence, not just productivity

Prioritize relational depth over procedural speed

Embed values like compassion, humility, and justice into their architecture

Allow clinicians to act with integrity, not just compliance

Recognize suffering not as a deviation, but as a central concern

AI can assist in this transformation. It can relieve administrative burdens, flag inequities, and surface patterns of harm. But it cannot define what matters. That task belongs to us.

To build a compassionate bureaucracy is to ask not only *what works*, but *what is right*. It is to design systems that do not silence the soul, but amplify it. Systems that do not just deliver care, but honor humanity.

IV. Designing for Ethical Attention

No matter how advanced AI in healthcare is, technical excellence alone is not enough. Accuracy, speed, and predictive power may enhance clinical performance—but they do not guarantee ethical care. To truly serve patients and clinicians, AI systems must be built with moral architecture: a design ethos that embeds empathy, equity, transparency, and narrative justice into every layer of the technology.

This is the heart of Designing for Ethical Attention—a commitment to systems that do not merely function, but *feel*. Systems that are attuned not only to data, but to the human experience behind it.

One robust framework for this is Value-Sensitive Design (VSD), developed by Friedman et al. (2002; 2019). VSD offers a structured, iterative approach that engages developers, clinicians, patients, and ethicists in a collaborative process. It integrates:

Conceptual analysis to identify core values at stake

Empirical inquiry to understand how those values manifest in real-world contexts

Technical implementation to embed those values into the system architecture

This approach ensures that technology reflects the shared moral landscape of those it serves—not just the priorities of efficiency or compliance.

Consider how this might look in practice:

Clinical dashboards that include patient quotes alongside lab results, reminding clinicians of the person behind the numbers

Decision prompts that ask about patient values before offering treatment plans, reframing care as a dialogue rather than a directive

System metrics that track relational continuity—how often a patient sees the same provider—not just task completion or throughput

These are not cosmetic changes. They are structural shifts. They signal that the system is designed not just to deliver care, but to honor relationship.

The goal is not merely system efficiency—it is system attunement. A healthcare environment where technology amplifies, rather than erodes, the clinician's capacity for empathy. Where algorithms support, rather than supplant, moral judgment. Where every design decision is a chance to ask: *Does this help us care better?*

Because in the end, ethical attention is not a feature. It is a foundation. And in building systems that reflect our deepest values, we do more than innovate—we humanize.

V. Institutional Mindfulness

To feel is not to abandon rigor. It is to balance rigor with resonance—to recognize that precision and empathy are not opposites, but partners in the pursuit of healing. In healthcare, this balance must extend beyond the individual clinician to the very systems in which they work. It calls for a new kind of organizational culture: one rooted in institutional mindfulness.

Institutional mindfulness is the deliberate cultivation of awareness, reflection, and ethical sensitivity at the structural level. It is a commitment to valuing not only clinical outcomes, but the emotional and moral textures of care. It asks institutions to listen—not just to metrics, but to meaning.

This kind of culture includes:

Reflective rounds for staff:

Spaces where clinicians can process emotional experiences, share ethical dilemmas, and reconnect with their purpose—without judgment or haste.

AI systems that track clinician fatigue patterns:

Not to penalize, but to protect. These systems can identify burnout risks and prompt supportive interventions, honoring the humanity of the healer.

Narrative patient feedback, not just numerical:

Stories, metaphors, and reflections that reveal what care *felt like*, not just what it *achieved*. These insights deepen understanding and guide improvement.

Structural accountability when systems create moral harm:

Mechanisms to recognize, address, and repair ethical injuries caused by bureaucratic pressures, algorithmic bias, or institutional neglect.

Institutional mindfulness is not a luxury. It is a necessity in an era where technology accelerates decision-making and compresses time. It ensures that as systems grow more intelligent, they also become more attuned to suffering, to complexity, to the soul of medicine.

Because when institutions feel—not emotionally, but ethically—they create space for clinicians to care with integrity. And in that space, healing becomes not just possible, but profound.

VI. Ritual Practice: Witness the System

Practice: Once a month, choose a system behavior (e.g., auto-documentation, diagnostic nudges, productivity dashboards) and ask:

"Whose values are being encoded here?"

“What kinds of care are being rewarded — or silenced?”

“How does this affect my capacity to be present, honest, or kind?”

Then: name one way to resist, reshape, or rehumanize that feature — even in a small way.

This practice fosters systems consciousness—a prerequisite for any physician who aspires to lead in the AI era.

VII. Dialogue: Physician ↔ AI ↔ patient

Physician → AI:

“Prioritize my next 15 patients based on complexity.”

AI → Physician:

“Priority list generated using comorbidity scores, recent visits, and flagged symptoms. Patient 7 deprioritized due to lack of documented red flags.”

Physician (inner voice):

“But Patient 7 lost her daughter last month. She’s not complex on paper — but she’s barely holding on.”

Patient → Physician:

“I thought maybe you forgot me.”

Physician:

“No system will ever tell me who matters most. You’re here. That’s what matters.”

VIII. Micro-Manifesto: The Ninth Key

I will see beyond what the system measures.

I will notice who is being left out.

I will question optimization when it silences care.

I will name the moral weight of design.

I will remember: A system cannot be healed if it cannot feel.

IX. Sacred prompt:

"How can I design a system that feels before it functions?"

Key 10: The Future

"To imagine the future, I must anchor deeper into the eternal."

Narrative Reflection (from the Future Physician Self)

I used to think the future was a horizon rushing toward us.

Now I know it is a mirror reflecting what we choose to become.

My students grew up with AI as a sibling, not a tool.

They speak fluently to machines and kindly to one another.

They do not fear automation — they fear apathy.

I once predicted medicine's evolution through algorithms.

But the deeper truth was quieter: technology advanced us,

yet tenderness sustained us.

The future was never a destination; it was an awakening.

And every time I slow down enough to imagine with hope,

the eternal answers back.

Clinical and Philosophical Conflict

The Encounter:

A group of medical students debates whether empathy will remain a clinical skill or become a nostalgic relic.

Their AI tutor projects outcomes proving that patient satisfaction can be maintained even without human touch.

The Conflict:

The data tempt them to efficiency; their hearts resist reduction.

They realize that meaning is not an outcome — it is a relationship.

The Philosophical Tension:

The future will not test whether machines can think,

but whether humans will still feel.

We build tomorrow every time we refuse to let prediction replace purpose.

I. Looking Ahead Without Losing Ourselves

The future of medicine is arriving faster than we can narrate it—drafted not solely by physicians, but by engineers, venture capitalists, bioethicists, policy-makers, and machine-learning models. AI is no longer speculative. It is embedded in triage systems, virtual assistants, decision support tools, and clinical documentation. The transformation is not coming. It is already here.

In this moment, the family physician stands at a crossroads. The choice is not merely technological—it is existential.

Adapt passively, or shape the future consciously.

To shape the future, we must look beyond metrics of efficiency and precision. We must ask more profound questions—questions that resist automation, that require moral imagination, that speak to the soul of medicine:

What kind of medicine do we want to practice in 10, 20, or 50 years?

Will it be transactional or relational? Mechanistic or humanistic? Will it honor complexity, or flatten it?

What kind of physicians do we hope to become?

Technicians of data, or stewards of care? Will we be guided by algorithms, or by empathy? Will we remember how to listen?

And most importantly: What will still matter when the machines can do almost everything we can?

Presence. Meaning. Trust. The ability to sit with suffering, to hold silence, to say "I'm here" when no solution exists.

These are not nostalgic questions. They are visionary ones. They invite us to reclaim medicine not just as a science, but as a moral practice. They remind us that the future is not something we inherit—it is something we design.

And if we design it well, we will not lose ourselves. We will find ourselves again—more deeply, more clearly, more human than ever.

II. Technological Forecasting and Its Limits

In public health and industry, predictive modeling and scenario planning are standard tools—used to anticipate trends, allocate resources, and prepare for disruption. Yet history reminds us that technological forecasting is a fragile art, often clouded by overconfidence and blind spots.

Experts underestimated the transformative power of the Internet, misread the trajectory of genomics, and overhyped the promise of nanotechnology. The lesson is clear: the future is not simply extrapolated from the past—it is imagined, shaped, and chosen.

This is where moral imagination becomes essential. It is not enough to predict what might happen. We must ask what *should* happen. What kind of future do we want to build—not just for systems, but for souls?

Amara's Law offers a sobering reminder: "We tend to overestimate the effect of a technology in the short run and underestimate its effect in the long run" (as cited in Cringely, 1991).

In the short term, AI may feel like a tool—streamlining documentation, triaging patients, optimizing workflows. But in the long term, it may reshape the very ethos of medicine: how we define care, how we relate to suffering, how we understand healing.

Thus, the wise physician must learn to think in both futures and eternals. To anticipate change, yes—but also to remain anchored in enduring human truths:

Relationship — the bond between healer and patient

Meaning — the search for coherence in illness

Presence — the gift of attention in suffering

Dignity — the affirmation of worth, even in decline

These are not relics of a pre-digital age. They are the compass points for navigating what comes next. And as AI continues to evolve, it is these truths—not just technical forecasts—that must guide the physician's path.

Because the future of medicine will not be defined solely by what machines can do. It will be defined by what humans choose to preserve, protect, and prioritize.

III. Educating the AI-Native Physician

Today's medical students are digital natives—fluent in apps, platforms, and cloud-based collaboration. But tomorrow's clinicians will be AI natives: entering practice in a world where intelligent systems are not add-ons, but foundations. They will never know medicine without voice-activated documentation, diagnostic prompting, or generative CME tools. For them, AI will not be a novelty—it will be the norm.

So what do they need most?

Not more information.

They will have access to more data than any generation before them. What they need is the capacity to navigate, interpret, and humanize that data. They need formation, not just instruction. They need:

Epistemic ethics

The ability to evaluate, question, and challenge AI outputs. To ask: *What assumptions shaped this recommendation? Whose values are embedded here?*

Narrative fluency

The skill to maintain patient storytelling in a data-dense world. To listen for meaning, not just metrics. To preserve the arc of a life amid the fragments of a chart.

Emotional literacy

The courage to name and navigate their own moral distress. To recognize when systems conflict with values, and to seek repair rather than retreat.

Systemic awareness

The insight to shape technologies rather than be shaped by them. To participate in design, policy, and governance—not just use the tools handed to them.

Existential courage

The strength to stand in uncertainty, not hide in models. To say "I don't know" with integrity. To accompany patients through ambiguity, not bypass it with prediction.

Medical education must therefore evolve—from content transmission to character formation. From memorizing facts to cultivating wisdom. From technical competence to moral imagination.

Because the AI-native physician will not just inherit a new toolkit, they will inherit a new terrain. And to navigate it well, they must be trained not only in what to do—but in who to be.

IV. Envisioning the Clinic Beyond 2030

Let us imagine a clinic transformed by technology—fluid, intelligent, and deeply responsive:

Ambient AI transcribes and analyzes each clinical encounter in real time, reducing documentation burden and surfacing insights as the conversation unfolds.

Digital twins simulate the patient's physiology, offering predictive models that anticipate complications before they arise.

Clinical dashboards visualize not only disease metrics, but patient values, goals, and narratives—making the person visible within the data.

Adaptive feedback loops offer live coaching to the clinician mid-encounter, refining communication, empathy, and decision-making in the moment.

Virtual rounds blend in-person, remote, and AI-curated insights, creating a collaborative, borderless model of care.

This is not science fiction. It is a plausible future that might happen sooner than we think—one already taking shape in research labs, pilot programs, and policy frameworks. But amid all this innovation, one truth must remain clear:

The heart of the clinic remains the same.

A patient in need.

A physician who cares.

We must not mistake technical augmentation for human irrelevance. The more intelligent our systems become, the more essential it is for physicians to be:

Emotionally intelligent — attuned to suffering, responsive to nuance

Spiritually grounded — able to hold meaning, mystery, and mortality

Ethically aware — capable of navigating complexity with integrity

Technology may guide the hand. But only the physician can hold the heart.

In the clinic of 2050, the tools will be extraordinary. But the healing will still depend on presence, relationship, and trust. And that is something no machine can replace.

V. Foresight as Moral Practice

Foresight is not prediction. It is an act of responsibility—a moral discipline that asks us to look ahead, not to forecast what *will* happen, but to shape what *ought* to happen. According to Slaughter (2004), foresight entails envisioning possible futures so that we may enact them with intention rather than inherit them by default.

In medicine, this practice becomes urgent. As I mentioned earlier, the future is being built not only by clinicians but also by technologists, corporations, and policymakers. The discipline of critical futures studies, as articulated by Sohail Inayatullah (1998), invites us to explore multiple futures—possible, probable, and preferable—while interrogating the values and assumptions that underlie each scenario.

For physicians, this means stepping beyond the clinical encounter and into the architecture of the future itself. It means:

Participating in tech policy, not just adapting to it. Physicians must have a seat at the table when decisions are made about AI integration, data governance, and digital ethics.

Advocating for ethical design and AI transparency. Clinicians must demand systems that are explainable, accountable, and aligned with human values—not just efficient.

Defending the role of relationship as central to healing. As technology accelerates, the relational core of medicine must not be lost. Presence, trust, and empathy are not optional—they are foundational.

Mentoring the next generation to be both tech-literate and soul-literate. Future physicians must be fluent in algorithms and attuned to meaning. They must know how to use tools—and how to remain human while doing so.

Foresight, then, is not a luxury. It is a moral imperative. It asks physicians to become architects of care, not just operators within it. It calls for vision, courage, and imagination. And it reminds us that the future of medicine will be shaped not only by what we build—but by what we choose to protect.

VI. Ritual Practice: Write the Letter

Practice: Write a letter to your future physician self — 20 years from now. Begin with:

"This is what I hope you have not forgotten..."

"This is what I hope you dared to protect..."

"This is how I hope you still show up for your patients..."

Seal it. Revisit it each year. Let it become your anchor and your compass.

VII. Dialogue: Physician ↔ AI ↔ patient

Physician → AI:

"Forecast this patient's 5-year risk for stroke and suggest the top 3 interventions by impact."

AI → Physician:

"Five-year stroke risk: 13.2%. Greatest impact interventions: anticoagulation initiation, BP optimization, lifestyle modification coaching."

Physician (inner reflection):

"And yet, he said he does not want to take one more pill — not after watching his father die in a hospital bed."

Patient → Physician:

"Doc, what would you do... if you were me?"

Physician:

"Let's talk about what matters most to you — not just the risk score."

VIII. Micro-Manifesto: The Tenth Key

I will not mistake the probable for the preferable.

I will educate for wisdom, not just competence.

I will imagine futures that center humanity.

I will stay rooted in what cannot be automated.

I will remember: To imagine the future,

I must anchor deeper into the eternal.

IX. Sacred prompt:

"What must remain sacred as I invent tomorrow's medicine?"

Key 11: The Disappearance

"One day, no one will remember my notes. Only how I made them feel."

Narrative Reflection (from the Future Physician Self)

I used to believe legacy was what remained after we were gone.

Now I understand it is what disappears within us while we are still here.

There will come a time when every chart I wrote will fade,

every protocol I created will be replaced.

Yet, in moments of stillness, I sense the quiet immortality

of those who once sat before me — their gratitude folded into time.

My AI archive holds every note I ever dictated,

but it cannot recall how my presence changed a room.

The record endures; the resonance outlives it.

Perhaps the goal was never to be remembered,

but to be felt so deeply that forgetting becomes impossible.

Clinical and Philosophical Conflict

<u>The Encounter:</u>

A retiring physician asks his AI assistant to summarize his lifetime of care.

The output: 82,000 visits, 11,400 prescriptions, 0.7% complication rate.

He stares at the numbers, then whispers, "But where are the people?"

<u>The Conflict:</u>

The AI captures achievement but not affection.

It measures the quantity of his touch, not the quality of his being.

The Philosophical Tension:

Disappearance is not erasure; it is integration.

The healer dissolves into the fabric of those once healed.

The most outstanding physicians do not leave monuments —

They leave a gentler world.

I. The Quiet Fade of Legacy

All physicians will disappear.

From their clinics, their roles, their EMRs. Their names will be removed from appointment books, dashboards will be cleared, and logins will be deactivated. The rhythms of their days—once so urgent—will dissolve into the quiet hum of systems that move on without them.

And even the most "efficient" clinician will not be remembered for how many notes they completed, how many boxes they checked, or how many protocols they followed.

They will be remembered, if at all, for how deeply they showed up.

In an age of AI permanence—where every interaction is recorded, tagged, and retrievable—it is tempting to believe that documentation is legacy. That which is stored will endure. But the truth is more subtle.

Presence leaves no record.

Compassion does not get coded.

Silence cannot be captured in a chart.

What endures is the residue of presence—the subtle but eternal imprint of dignity, kindness, and attention. A hand held in fear. A pause before truth.

A moment of shared humanity that lives on not in data, but in memory, in meaning, in the quiet transformation of those who were witnessed.

This is the disappearance.

Not a failure.

But the healer's final humility.

To care deeply, knowing you will be forgotten.

To show up fully, knowing your name will fade.

To leave behind not a legacy of metrics, but a legacy of presence.

And in that fading, something sacred remains.

II. Ego and the Physician Identity

Modern medical culture, especially under the growing pressure of AI comparisons, subtly encourages physicians to preserve ego through performance metrics and productivity benchmarks. The culture whispers:

"I caught that rare diagnosis."

"I finished all my notes in real-time."

"I ranked top in diagnostic accuracy."

These affirmations are not inherently wrong. They reflect dedication, skill, and discipline. But when identity becomes tethered solely to output, we risk building a self that cannot withstand disappearance—the inevitable fading from roles, records, and recognition.

In the framework of Erik Erikson's generativity versus stagnation stage (1950), healthy adults seek to foster projects, relationships, and values that outlive them. Not for glory, but to enrich others' lives. For physicians, this means shifting from a focus on personal achievement to a legacy of impact and influence.

It means:

Teaching not just facts, but wisdom

Mentoring with presence, not just precision

Creating systems that care, not just perform

Balancing information with intimacy, so that knowledge serves connection—not replaces it.

In an era where AI may outperform humans in speed, recall, and pattern recognition, the physician's identity must evolve. Not by competing with machines, but by deepening what machines cannot touch: empathy, meaning, and moral imagination.

To be a physician is not just to know—it is to become. And what we become is measured not by dashboards, but by the lives we've touched, the values we've lived, and the humanity we've preserved.

That is the ego worth cultivating. One that can disappear quietly—and leave behind something eternal.

III. Teaching Without Imposing

As AI begins to train itself by watching physicians work—recording gestures, parsing speech, analyzing decisions—a new temptation arises: to leave an imprint on the machine. To shape its logic, its outputs, its clinical style. To believe that our legacy will be encoded in algorithms.

But the more profound legacy may not be what your AI learns from you.

It may be what your student does when no one is watching.

The tone they use.

The eye contact they offer.

The stories they remember.

The silence they honor.

These are not technical skills. They are moral inheritances—passed not through lectures, but through presence. They are the subtle transmissions that shape a healer's soul.

This echoes Paulo Freire's *Pedagogy of the Oppressed* (1970), which insists that education should liberate, not deposit knowledge. In Freire's view, true teaching is not about control—it is about awakening. It is about helping learners become more fully themselves, not more perfectly you.

So, in the AI era, mentorship must evolve. It must go beyond technique to transmit:

Ethics — the ability to discern right action in complexity.

Presence — the capacity to be fully with another, even in suffering.

Humility — the strength to say "I don't know," and still show up.

Your best teaching will never be in your presentations.

It will be in your way of being.

In how you pause.

In how you listen.

In how you treat the patient when no one else is in the room.

AI may learn your patterns. But your students will carry your values.

And that is the legacy that matters most.

IV. The Wisdom of Letting Go

In Eastern traditions—notably Buddhism and Taoism—the practice of non-attachment is not indifference. It is wisdom. It is the ability to engage fully without clinging to control, recognition, or permanence. For physicians, this wisdom is essential.

To care deeply without needing to be needed.

To act skillfully without needing to be right.

To show up fully without needing to be remembered.

To speak truth without needing the final word.

These are not acts of resignation. They are acts of moral maturity.

This practice finds resonance in Roshi Joan Halifax's model of "edge states"—altruism, empathy, integrity, respect, and engagement. These are not fragile virtues. They are sources of moral strength that allow caregivers to sustain compassion without being consumed by outcomes (Halifax, 2018). They offer a way to remain present without grasping, to serve without ego, to heal without attachment.

As AI begins to outperform us in certain technical domains—diagnostic speed, data synthesis, predictive modeling—our strength will lie elsewhere.

It will lie in what cannot be measured:

The quiet dignity of presence

The grace of uncertainty

The humility to step back when the time comes

Letting go is not failure. It is the physician's final wisdom.

To know that the most profound impact may leave no trace.

To trust that compassion, once offered, does not need to be remembered to endure.

V. Ritual Practice: The Anonymous Gift

Practice: Once a month, offer something in your work that no one will trace to you — a kind note, an extra moment with a grieving family, a call to a patient who was not scheduled, a thank-you to a staff member.

Do it without announcing, logging, or tracking it.

Let it disappear — like a seed into soil.

This is the practice of ego-shedding. It teaches you to give without needing to be seen.

VI. Dialogue: Physician ↔ AI ↔ patient

Physician → AI:

"Draft a mentorship evaluation for my resident."

AI → Physician:

"Dr. Lee demonstrates strong diagnostic reasoning, effective communication, and timely documentation. Likely to succeed in academic or clinical practice."

Physician (inner voice):

"But what I hope they carry isn't in this text. It's how they held that patient's hand when the diagnosis was crushing."

Patient → Physician:

"I don't remember your name... but I remember how you looked at me. Like I mattered."

Physician:

"That's enough."

VII. Micro-Manifesto: The Eleventh Key

I will not seek to be remembered.

I will practice as though my legacy is in the next gesture.

I will let go of the need to be right or recognized.

I will disappear with grace, but not before transmitting light.

I will remember: One day, no one will remember my notes.

Only how I made them feel.

VIII. Sacred prompt:

"If only my presence could remain, what would it whisper when I am gone?"

Key 12: The Return

"I was never replaced. I remembered who I was."

Narrative Reflection (from the Future Physician Self)

The circle is complete.

I began this journey afraid of obsolescence; I end it astonished by renewal.

The AI still works beside me — wiser, faster, quieter — yet no longer a rival.

It has become a witness to my becoming.

I once searched for what made me indispensable.

Now I simply live what makes me irreplaceable: compassion, wonder, imperfection, grace.

The machine remembers everything; I remember what matters.

In our partnership, I found not the end of humanity,

but its deeper beginning.

Clinical and Philosophical Conflict

The Encounter:

A final-year resident asks, "If AI can think faster, diagnose earlier, and never forget, what's left for us?"

The Conflict:

I invite her to hold a patient's trembling hand.

The room fills with presence; the question answers itself.

The Philosophical Tension:

The Return is not a retreat to the past, but a restoration of meaning.

We built machines to mirror us — and found ourselves mirrored back.

To return is to recognize that the purpose of intelligence,

human or artificial, is not domination but devotion.

I. Full Circle

This book began with a prompt—a question cast outward into the future. It ends with a return—an invitation inward.

After journeying through the edges of technology, the depths of presence, the weight of story, and the quiet inevitability of disappearance, we arrive not at supremacy, but at sovereignty. Not domination over machines, but integration of the self. The physician of the future is not the one who knows the most, but the one who knows who they are—and shows up whole.

AI may augment thought, language, and even simulate empathy. It may assist, accelerate, and advise. But the return is not about AI. It is about remembering.

Remembering what no intelligence—artificial or otherwise—can replicate:

The inner coherence of being fully human.

The quiet strength of presence.

The moral clarity of care.

The soul behind the science.

This is the full circle.

Not a conclusion, but a beginning.

Not a solution, but a stance.

A way of being that holds space for both innovation and intimacy.

A future shaped not just by what we build, but by who we choose to become.

II. The Journey: Twelve Doors of Becoming

Each chapter of this book was not just an idea, but a threshold. Together, they represent a map of return—a movement back to the physician's actual presence.

Key	What Was Reclaimed
1. The Question	Epistemic humility
2. The Mirror	Self-awareness
3. The Twin	Identity stewardship
4. The Threshold	Ethical accompaniment
5. The Narrative	Story as healing
6. The Presence	Attention as care
7. The Limit	Action amid uncertainty
8. The Soul	Meaning beyond medicine
9. The System	Moral design
10. The Future	Purpose in vision
11. The Disappearance	Grace in legacy
12. The Return	Wholeness in selfhood

You are not just practicing medicine. You are becoming it.

III. AI as Companion, Not Core

I think you already recognize that as AI becomes more ambient, more integrated, and more "intelligent," the boundaries between physician and machine may begin to blur. Predictive models increasingly shape clinical decisions. Documentation flows from voice. Diagnostic suggestions arrive before the stethoscope touches skin. In this landscape, it can feel complex—sometimes disorienting—to know where the physician ends and the machine begins.

Let us repeat what we said earlier to be clear:

The machine can assist.

It can advise.

It can amplify.

But it cannot decide who you are.

You are the final integrator—not because you compute faster, but because you hold what no algorithm can:

Context — the lived reality of the patient before you

Memory — the continuity of care across time and story

Responsibility — the moral weight of decisions that affect lives

Ethical agency — the capacity to discern, to feel, to choose

You bear witness to pain.

You navigate paradox.

You offer presence when no outcome can be guaranteed.

Again, this is not anti-technology. This is post-technology—a maturity that allows us to wield tools without being consumed by them. It is the wisdom to use AI not as a replacement, but as a companion. To let it extend our reach, but not define our role.

In this future, the physician remains essential—not because they outperform machines, but because they embody humanity. And that is something no system can simulate.

IV. The Return to the Sacred

The word "clinic" derives from the Greek klinein, meaning "to lean." To be a clinician, then, is not merely to diagnose or treat, but to lean toward: toward suffering, toward mystery, toward the unknown. It is a posture of presence, a gesture of humility, a movement toward what cannot be solved but must still be witnessed.

This return is not technological.

It is spiritual—not necessarily religious, but undeniably sacred.

It is a return to:

Slowness in a world that rushes:

Making space for breath, for silence, for the unhurried unfolding of story.

Embodiment in a culture that abstracts:

Remembering that healing happens not in data points, but in bodies, in touch, in shared humanity.

Wisdom in a system that automates:

Holding discernment above efficiency, and meaning above metrics.

Compassion in an era of calculation:

Choosing to care even when it's not cost-effective, to feel even when it's not required.

And most importantly:

A return to yourself.

To the part of you that chose medicine not for mastery, but for mystery.

To the part that knows healing is not a transaction, but a relationship.

To the part that leans—not away from suffering, but toward it.

This is the sacred center of care.

And in returning to it, we do not regress.

We remember.

V. Ritual Practice: The Annual Vow

Practice: Once a year — on your birthday, the anniversary of your graduation, or a day of your choosing — recite aloud your vow as a physician.

It need not be long. It must be real. Consider beginning with:

"I still believe...

That what matters most is not what I do, but how I do it.

That even if machines aid me, I must never act like one.

That each patient is a mystery—and a mirror.

That my presence is more potent than my productivity.

That I am here to witness, not just to fix.

That the last human touch will always matter — even if no one remembers my name."

VI. Dialogue: Physician ↔ AI ↔ patient

AI → Physician:

"Would you like me to summarize your last 10 years of cases?"

Physician:

"No. I remember the ones that mattered."

Patient → Physician:

"You probably don't remember me. But when my daughter was dying, you sat with us. You didn't say much. But it changed everything."

Physician (after a long pause):

"I remember. Thank you for coming back."

VII. Micro-Manifesto: The Twelfth Key

I will not outsource who I am.

I will let the machine assist, but not define me.

I will return — again and again — to meaning, presence, and truth.

I will meet complexity with wholeness.

I will walk into the future with humility, not haste.

I will remember: I was never replaced.

I remembered who I was.

VIII. Sacred prompt:

"What does it mean to remember myself fully while walking beside the machine?"

Afterword: The Healer Beyond the Machine

"The future is not something we enter. It is something we shape."

— Leonard Sweet

This book began with a single paradox: that in an age of machine intelligence, what makes us most human becomes *most vital.* You have now walked through twelve keys — each one opening a deeper layer of clinical life, not by opposing AI, but by transcending its limits.

What you carry now is not a manual.

It is *a map of becoming* — a way to remain both grounded and visionary, both data-literate and soul-attuned, both precise and present.

You are not just a physician.

You are *a witness, a weaver*, and at times, *a warrior* — standing at the convergence of technology and tenderness.

Let the world grow faster.

You will remain *anchored.*

Let the algorithms grow smarter.

You will grow *wiser.*

Let systems change.

You will stay *human.*

The last human touch was never at risk of extinction.

It was simply waiting — for someone like you — to return to it.

With reverence,

Abdullah Al Ghamdi, MD

Family Physician

Appendices

Appendix A: Sacred Prompt Templates

These prompts are designed not for speed, but for depth, truth, and ethical clarity.

For Diagnosis:

"What diagnosis would I least want to miss — and why?"

"What alternative explanations are emotionally harder to face?"

For Decision-Making:

"What is this patient not saying that I should still hear?"

"What would I do if this were a loved one?"

For Teaching:

"What questions will deepen their character, not just their competence?"

"What am I modeling right now — and is it worth inheriting?"

For Reflection:

"What part of this encounter moved me?"

"What would my AI never understand about what just happened?"

Appendix B: The Presence Inventory

A simple weekly journal tool.

Prompt	Your Reflection
One moment this week, I truly showed up.	
One moment I missed — and why	
What I felt in my body during a difficult encounter	
A question I asked that led to an unexpected truth	
What I am learning about being with suffering	

This inventory is not for performance.

It is for *remembering who you are becoming*.

Appendix C: The Physician's Annual Vow Template

Create your own, or use the guided version:

"I vow to remain present, even when it hurts.

I vow to question what feels automated.

I vow to listen beyond words, beyond charts, beyond algorithms.

I vow to protect what cannot be replaced: story, dignity, silence, trust.

I vow to remember why I began — and who I hope to become."

Date it. Sign it. Repeat annually.

Companion CME / Teaching Toolkit

3-Day Workshop Curriculum

The Last Human Touch: Practicing Medicine Beyond AI

A Reflective Masterclass in Humanism, Technology, and Healing

1. Purpose and Rationale

This workshop translates the twelve Keys of The Last Human Touch into an experiential learning sequence that strengthens physicians' reflective capacity, ethical reasoning, and presence in an AI-augmented world.

Participants move through three progressive domains:

Day	Domain	Focus	Educational Goal
Day 1 – Awareness	Self	Understanding how AI mirrors human cognition and bias	Know thy mirror
Day 2 – Relationship	Patient	Reclaiming narrative empathy and moral presence	Heal through attention
Day 3 – Renewal	System	Re-humanizing healthcare structures and leadership	Design systems that can feel

Each day integrates four Keys, linking conceptual discussion, reflective writing, group dialogue, and embodied presence.

2. Theoretical Foundations

Theory	Application in Curriculum
Kolb's Experiential Learning Cycle (1984)	Every session includes experience → reflection → conceptualization → experimentation loops.
Mezirow's Transformative Learning (1991)	Participants question assumptions about technology and reframe professional identity.
Schön's Reflective Practitioner (1983)	Structured "mirror moments" for reflection-in-action during clinical simulations.
Vygotsky's Social Constructivism	Knowledge co-created through peer dialogue and triadic interactions (Physician ↔ AI ↔ Patient).
Knowles' Andragogy (1980)	Adult learners lead their inquiry; facilitators serve as guides.
Dewey's Pragmatism	Reflection translated into concrete workplace rituals and micro-manifestos.

3. Curriculum Design Principles

Accessibility: Requires only a whiteboard, printed excerpts, and an optional AI interface (phone/tablet).

Human-Centered Pedagogy: Learning arises from lived experience, not abstract instruction.

Triadic Dialogue Framework: Every discussion triangulates human, machine, and moral perspectives.

Ritual Learning: Each day closes with a symbolic act anchoring reflection in embodied memory.

Outcome Integration: Cognitive (knowledge), Affective (empathy), Behavioral (practice).

4. Schedule Overview (3 Days × 8 hours = 24 contact hours)

Day	Focused Keys	Theme	Expected Transformation
Day 1 – Awareness: "The Mirror of Knowing"	Keys 1–4 (The Question, The Mirror, The Twin, The Threshold)	From automation to self-awareness	Physicians recognize AI as a mirror of their cognition and bias.
Day 2 – Relationship: "The Space Between"	Keys 5–8 (The Narrative, The Presence, The Limit, The Soul)	From efficiency to empathy	Physicians rediscover slow attention and narrative humility.
Day 3 – Renewal: "The Future That Feels"	Keys 9–12 (The System, The Future, The Disappearance, The Return)	From institution to inspiration	Physicians design humane systems and personal rituals for sustainable practice.

5. Detailed Daily Curriculum

DAY 1 – The Mirror of Knowing

Objective: Build awareness of how AI reveals, amplifies, or distorts the physician's thinking and moral stance.

Relevant Theories: Kolb (reflection cycle), Schön (reflection-in-action), Knowles (self-directed learning)

Morning (4 hours)

Time	Activity	Method	Outcome
08:00–08:30	Opening Ritual – "The Pulse Check"	Guided breathing + intention journaling	Psychological safety, group attunement
08:30–09:30	Micro-Lecture 1: The Question as an Ethical Act	Interactive talk + case vignette	Recognize moral dimensions of AI use
09:30–10:30	Triadic Dialogue 1: Physician ↔ AI ↔ Patient	Role-play (paper scripts)	Identify tensions between efficiency and empathy
10:45–12:00	Reflective Writing 1: My First Mirror Moment	Individual writing + pair sharing	Awareness of bias and emotional response

Afternoon (4 hours)

Time	Activity	Method	Outcome
13:00–14:30	Case Workshop: The Cognitive Twin	Group analysis of real clinical AI cases	Critical appraisal of machine reasoning
14:30–15:30	Mini-Lecture 2: Crossing the Threshold of Ambiguity	Discussion-based lecture	Tolerate uncertainty in diagnosis
15:45–16:30	Presence Practice 1: 3-minute silent observation of patient video	Embodied exercise	Cultivate attentional stillness
16:30–17:00	Closing Circle: "One Line of Realization"	Oral sharing	Collective synthesis

Low-resource adaptation: Replace AI interface with printed algorithm summaries; use local case studies instead of digital simulation.

DAY 2 – The Space Between

Objective: Deepen relational intelligence through narrative reflection, compassion practices, and awareness of human limits.

Relevant Theories: Mezirow (transformative learning), Charon (narrative medicine), Vygotsky (social dialogue)

Morning (4 hours)

Time	Activity	Method	Outcome
08:00–08:20	Ritual: "Lighting the Story"	Reading from Key 5 – The Narrative	Emotional centering
08:20–09:00	Mini-Lecture 3: The Story as Clinical Data	Interactive presentation	Understand narrative reasoning
09:00–10:00	Narrative Writing Lab 1	Prompt from workbook	Convert patient memory into meaning
10:15–12:00	Peer Dialogue: When the Note Forgets the Soul	Small groups	Recognize loss of personhood through automation

Afternoon (4 hours)

Time	Activity	Method	Outcome
13:00–14:30	Workshop: Practicing Slow Medicine	Guided mindfulness + simulated encounter	Re-embody presence
14:30–15:30	Mini-Lecture 4: The Limit and the Soul	Socratic dialogue	Embrace humility and mortality
15:45–16:30	Micro-Manifesto Lab 1	Writing + calligraphy	Articulate ethical commitments
16:30–17:00	Evening Reflection: "Two Lines of Gratitude"	Journaling	Integrate compassion fatigue insights

Low-resource adaptation: Replace patient actors with peer role-play; mindfulness done seated; use printed stories if screens are unavailable.

DAY 3 – The Future That Feels

Objective: Integrate personal reflection into institutional and systemic renewal.

Relevant Theories: Dewey (experiential pragmatism), Wenger (communities of practice), Mezirow (action → transformation)

Morning (4 hours)

Time	Activity	Method	Outcome
08:00–08:15	Opening Ritual: "Threshold of Return"	Collective silence	Transition awareness
08:15–09:15	Mini-Lecture 5: Systems That Can Feel	Case + design thinking	Human-centered system redesign
09:15–11:00	Design Lab 1: The Compassionate Workflow	Group project	Prototype a humane clinic ritual
11:15–12:00	Reflection Writing III: The Physician's Promise to Tomorrow	Individual journaling	Define moral identity in future medicine

Afternoon (4 hours)

Time	Activity	Method	Outcome
13:00–14:30	Peer Presentations: Twelve Keys in Twelve Voices	Story sharing	Collective integration of learning
14:30–15:30	Mini-Lecture 6: The Return as Renewal	Brief talk + discussion	Sustain reflection as a lifelong habit
15:45–16:45	Closing Ritual: "The Last Human Touch"	Symbolic group gesture	Emotional closure, community bond
16:45–17:00	Evaluation & Commitment	Self-assessment + feedback	Map post-workshop growth plan

Low-resource adaptation: System design projects can be drawn on flip charts; rituals may use local cultural symbols (dates, candles, prayer mats, etc.).

6. Learning Resources

The Last Human Touch (core text)

Reflective Workbook (one per participant)

Basic stationery (A4 pads, pens, index cards)

Timer or phone for mindfulness cues

Optional laptop/tablet for AI demonstrations

7. Evaluation Framework (Kirkpatrick Model)

Level	Tool	Indicator
1 – Reaction	End-of-day "Pulse Word" survey	Engagement, relevance
2 – Learning	Reflective essay rubric	Depth of insight, conceptual accuracy
3 – Behavior	30-day follow-up reflection	Evidence of changed practice
4 – Results	Institutional story submission	Adoption of rituals, team dialogue

8. Expected Outputs

By workshop end, each participant will have:

A Personal Micro-Manifesto (ethical compass).

A Reflective Case Narrative demonstrating integration of AI and empathy.

A Prototype "Human Touch Ritual" for their workplace.

A Peer Community of Practice for continued reflection.

9. Scalability and Resource Adaptation

Setting	Adaptation
Academic Hospitals	Integrate into faculty-development or resident well-being programs.
Primary-Care Clinics	Deliver as half-day modules over 3 weeks.
Rural / Low-tech Environments	Use printed cards, verbal prompts, and hand-written reflections; replace AI demos with analog ethical dilemmas.

10. Closing Educational Philosophy

Machines may calculate care, but only humans consecrate it.

This curriculum ensures that every physician leaves not merely trained in reflection, but transformed by remembering what only the human hand can hold.

Reflective Workbook

For Medical Students, Residents, and Early-Career Physicians Studying

The Last Human Touch

Purpose

This workbook adapts the themes and rituals of *The Last Human Touch* into a practical, guided journal for physicians-in-training. It promotes identity formation, ethical resilience, emotional literacy, and conscious use of AI in clinical life.

Ideal for:

Undergraduate medical education (UME)

Residency onboarding

Faculty mentorship circles

Burnout prevention workshops

Structure of the Workbook

Each chapter = one Key from the book.

Each chapter includes:

Anchor Quote

Reflection Prompt

Patient Encounter Memory Prompt

Mirror Moment (Self-Confrontation)

AI Reframing Task

Presence Practice

Mini-Manifesto Box

Sample Chapter Template

Key 3: *The Twin*

Theme: Boundaries, Memory, and Moral Personalization

Purpose

This sample chapter is offered as a guide and invitation, not a prescription.

It demonstrates how you, the reflective reader or educator, can translate any of the twelve Keys from *The Last Human Touch* into your own living chapter — one that blends your story, your patients, and your evolving dialogue with AI.

You are encouraged to adapt this framework as you see fit for each Key that speaks to you.

Use this example from *Key 3: The Twin* as a model to design your own templates for *The Question, The Mirror, The Threshold,* and beyond.

Each one will differ — because no two physicians, no two reflections, and no two thresholds of becoming are ever the same.

The form is here to serve your awareness, not to limit it.

1. Anchor Quote

"Who is writing this note — the physician, or the system?"

(Optional alternates for educators)

"Every mirror reflects a truth the eye alone cannot see."

"The twin remembers, but the human forgives."

Pause here. Breathe. Read the quote aloud. Let it echo before you write.

2. Reflection Prompt

When you use an AI assistant — to summarize, draft, diagnose, or decide — what happens inside you?

Are you learning, or outsourcing your discernment?

Write a few lines about a moment when you caught yourself surrendering not just the task, but the thinking behind it.

Then ask: *What was I afraid to face — error, effort, or uncertainty?*

3. Patient Encounter Memory

Recall a patient you saw recently whose care was shaped by AI input — a risk score, a draft note, or a decision tree.

How did the tool alter your perception of the patient?

What did it clarify, and what did it obscure?

Write a brief story (150–200 words). Begin not with the diagnosis, but with the silence before you spoke.

4. Mirror Moment *(Self-Confrontation)*

Look inward.

What part of yourself did the AI reflect— your efficiency, your bias, your exhaustion?

Circle one that feels most confronting. Then, write freely for five minutes about how that quality shapes your clinical judgment.

Finish the reflection with this line:

"My twin reminds me that..."

(Example: "My twin reminds me that precision without patience is still a form of blindness.")

5. AI Reframing Task

Ask your AI companion this prompt directly, or imagine its answer:

"What are three ways physicians over-rely on algorithms in primary care?"

Now, respond to it — not as a user, but as a mentor writing to a curious apprentice.

If the AI were human, what would you want it to learn from you about compassion, risk, and restraint?

<u>6. Presence Practice</u>

In your subsequent clinic encounter, resist entering any data for the first three minutes.

Just observe — the tone, the breathing, the small gestures that no system captures.

Afterward, return to this page and write two short lines:

What shifted in the patient?

What shifted in me?

Note: If you feel restless during those three minutes, that is your signal — presence has begun its work.

<u>7. Mini-Manifesto Box</u>

Write a three-line vow you can return to daily:

I will listen to...

I will question when...

I will stay human by...

(Leave room to sign and date it.)

Revisit this page in three months. Has your twin changed—or have you?

Notes for Educators and Facilitators

This exercise works best in silence, or after a shared reading from *The Last Human Touch*.

Encourage story before analysis — experience before abstraction.

For group sessions, close with each participant reading their Mini-Manifesto aloud (one line at a time).

The room becomes its own mirror.

Closing Note

The twin remembers; the healer awakens.

Each reflection is not a task to finish, but a door to re-enter.

When you write, you are not documenting your past —

You are designing your conscience.

Bibliography

Balboni, M. J., Sullivan, A., Enzinger, A. C., Epstein-Peterson, Z. D., Tseng, Y. D., Mitchell, C., ... & Balboni, T. A. (2014). Nurse and physician barriers to spiritual care provision at the end of life. *Journal of Pain and Symptom Management, 48*(3), 400–410. https://doi.org/10.1016/j.jpainsymman.2013.09.020

Bruner, J. (1986). *Actual minds, possible worlds*. Harvard University Press.

Buber, M. (1958). *I and Thou* (R. G. Smith, Trans.). Charles Scribner's Sons.

Burrell, J. (2016). How the machine 'thinks': Understanding opacity in machine learning algorithms. *Big Data & Society, 3*(1), 1–12. https://doi.org/10.1177/2053951715622512

Charon, R. (2006). *Narrative medicine: Honoring the stories of illness*. Oxford University Press.

Clark, A., & Chalmers, D. (1998). The extended mind. *Analysis, 58*(1), 7–19. https://doi.org/10.1093/analys/58.1.7

Craig, A. D. (2002). How do you feel? Interoception: the sense of the physiological condition of the body. *Nature Reviews Neuroscience, 3*(8), 655–666. https://doi.org/10.1038/nrn894

Cringely, R. X. (1991). *Accidental Empires: How the Boys of Silicon Valley Make Their Millions, Battle Foreign Competition, and Still Can't Get a Date.* Addison-Wesley.

Croskerry, P. (2009). A universal model of diagnostic reasoning. *Academic Medicine, 84*(8), 1022–1028. https://doi.org/10.1097/ACM.0b013e3181ace703

Cruess, R. L., Cruess, S. R., Boudreau, J. D., Snell, L., & Steinert, Y. (2014). Reframing medical education to support professional identity formation.

Academic Medicine, 89(11), 1446–1451. https://doi.org/10.1097/ACM.0000000000000427

Dane, E. (2010). Reconsidering the trade-off between expertise and flexibility: A cognitive entrenchment perspective. *Academy of Management Review, 35*(4), 579–603. https://doi.org/10.5465/amr.2010.53502672

Engel, G. L. (1977). The need for a new medical model: A challenge for biomedicine. *Science, 196*(4286), 129–136. https://doi.org/10.1126/science.847460

Epstein, E. G., & Hamric, A. B. (2009). Moral distress, moral residue, and the crescendo effect. *The Journal of Clinical Ethics, 20*(4), 330–342.

Erikson, E. H. (1950). *Childhood and society.* W. W. Norton.

Frankl, V. E. (1946). *Man's Search for Meaning.* Beacon Press.

Freire, P. (1970). *Pedagogy of the Oppressed.* New York: Herder and Herder.

Friedman, B., & Hendry, D. G. (2019). *Value Sensitive Design: Shaping Technology with Moral Imagination.* MIT Press.

Friedman, B., Kahn, P. H., & Borning, A. (2002). Value Sensitive Design: Theory and Methods. *University of Washington Technical Report.*

Gadamer, H.-G. (1975). *Truth and method.* Continuum.

Gilligan, C. (1982). *In a different voice: Psychological theory and women's development.* Harvard University Press.

Hafferty, F. W. (1998). Beyond curriculum reform: Confronting medicine's hidden curriculum. *Academic Medicine, 73*(4), 403–407. https://doi.org/10.1097/00001888-199804000-00013

Halifax, J. (2018). *Standing at the Edge: Finding Freedom Where Fear and Courage Meet.* Flatiron Books.

Immordino-Yang, M. H., McColl, A., Damasio, H., & Damasio, A. (2009). Neural correlates of admiration and compassion. *Proceedings of the National*

Academy of Sciences of the United States of America, 106(19), 8021–8026. https://doi.org/10.1073/pnas.0810363106

Inayatullah, S. (1998). Causal layered analysis: Poststructuralism as method. *Futures, 30*(8), 815–829. https://doi.org/10.1016/S0016-3287(98)00086-X

Kabat-Zinn, J. (1990). *Full catastrophe living: Using the wisdom of your body and mind to face stress, pain, and illness*. Delacorte.

Kahneman, D. (2011). *Thinking, fast and slow*. Farrar, Straus and Giroux.

Kay, J. (2001). Learner control. *User Modeling and User-Adapted Interaction, 11*(1–2), 111–127. https://doi.org/10.1023/A:1011145532042

Keats, J. (1958). *The letters of John Keats, 1814–1821* (H. E. Rollins, Ed., Vol. 1). Harvard University Press. (Original work written 1817)

Koenig, H. G. (2012). Religion, spirituality, and health: The research and clinical implications. *ISRN Psychiatry, 2012*, 278730. https://doi.org/10.5402/2012/278730

Konkin, J., Grave, L., Cockburn, E., & Walters, L. (2020). Exploration of rural physicians' lived experience of practising outside their usual scope of practice to provide access to essential medical care (clinical courage): An international phenomenological study. *BMJ Open, 10*(8), e037705. https://doi.org/10.1136/bmjopen-2020-037705

Levinas, E. (1969). *Totality and infinity: An essay on exteriority* (A. Lingis, Trans.). Duquesne University Press.

Magolda, M. B. B. (2004). *Making their own way: Narratives for transforming higher education to promote self-development*. Stylus Publishing.

Montgomery, K. (2006). *How doctors think: Clinical judgment and the practice of medicine*. Oxford University Press. https://doi.org/10.1093/oso/9780195187120.001.0001

Mount, B., & Kearney, M. (2003). Healing and palliative care: charting our way forward. *Palliative Medicine*, 17(8), 657-658. https://doi.org/10.1191/0269216303pm848ed

Nussbaum, M. C. (2011). *Creating capabilities: The human development approach.* Harvard University Press.

Pasquale, F. (2015). *The Black Box Society: The Secret Algorithms That Control Money and Information.* Cambridge, MA: Harvard University Press.

Price, W. N., & Cohen, I. G. (2019). Privacy in the age of medical big data. *Nature Medicine, 25,* 37–43. https://doi.org/10.1038/s41591-018-0272-7

Reynolds, S. J. (2008). Moral attentiveness: Who pays attention to the moral aspects of life? *Journal of Applied Psychology, 93*(5), 1027–1041. https://doi.org/10.1037/0021-9010.93.5.1027

Rogers, C. R. (1961). *On becoming a person: A therapist's view of psychotherapy.* Houghton Mifflin.

Rosa, H. (2013). *Social Acceleration: A New Theory of Modernity.* Columbia University Press.

Schön, D. A. (1983). *The reflective practitioner: How professionals think in action.* Basic Books.

Slaughter, R. A. (2004). *Futures Beyond Dystopia: Creating Social Foresight.* RoutledgeFalmer.

Stewart, M., Brown, J. B., Donner, A., McWhinney, I. R., Oates, J., Weston, W. W., & Jordan, J. (2000). The impact of patient-centered care on outcomes. *The Journal of Family Practice, 49*(9), 796–804.

Toombs, S. K. (1993). *The meaning of illness: A phenomenological account of the different perspectives of physician and patient.* Kluwer Academic Publishers.

Turner, V. (1969). *The Ritual Process: Structure and Anti-Structure.* Aldine Publishing.

Tversky, A., & Kahneman, D. (1981). The framing of decisions and the psychology of choice. *Science, 211*(4481), 453–458. https://doi.org/10.1126/science.7455683

van Dijck, J. (2014). Datafication, dataism and dataveillance: Big Data between scientific paradigm and ideology. *Surveillance & Society*, *12*(2), 197–208. https://doi.org/10.24908/ss.v12i2.4776

Whitcomb, D., Battaly, H., Baehr, J., & Howard-Snyder, D. (2017). *Intellectual humility: Owning our limitations. Philosophy and Phenomenological Research, 94*(3), 509–539. https://doi.org/10.1111/phpr.12228

Whitcomb, D., Battaly, H., Baehr, J., & Howard-Snyder, D. (2017). Intellectual humility: Owning our limitations. *Philosophy and Phenomenological Research*, 94(3), 509-539. https://doi.org/10.1111/phpr.12228

Young, I. M. (2011). *Responsibility for Justice*. Oxford University Press. https://doi.org/10.1093/acprof:oso/9780195392388.001.0001

Zagzebski, L. T. (1996). *Virtues of the mind: An inquiry into the nature of virtue and the ethical foundations of knowledge*. Cambridge University Press.

About the Author

Dr. Abdullah Al Ghamdi is a consultant family physician based in Riyadh, Saudi Arabia. With over two decades of experience in clinical medicine, medical education, research, and leadership, he has devoted his career to patient-centered care, innovation, and the advancement of family medicine.

Dr. Al Ghamdi holds advanced degrees in Leading Innovation and Change (York St John University, UK) and in Health Professions Education (Maastricht University, Netherlands), as well as certifications in Health Informatics and Executive Physician Leadership. He is a Fellow of the College of Family Physicians of Canada and a Certified Physician Executive. His expertise spans clinical family medicine, addiction medicine, digital health, knowledge management, and AI-driven healthcare transformation.

He has served in senior leadership roles, including Associate Deputy Executive Director for Clinical Affairs and Corporate Director of Public Relations and Media Affairs at King Abdulaziz Medical City–Riyadh, where he led the successful implementation of one of the region's most advanced electronic medical record systems. His leadership has been recognized with multiple awards, including honors from the CEO of the Ministry of National Guard Health Affairs and a spot on the Top 100 Healthcare Leaders worldwide list at the International Forum on Advancements in Healthcare in 2019.

Alongside his leadership work, Dr. Al Ghamdi served as Adjunct Assistant Professor of Family Medicine at King Saud bin Abdulaziz University for Health Sciences. He has supervised numerous research projects, contributed to scholarly publications, and lectured at international conferences.

Through his writing, Dr. Al Ghamdi brings together his clinical wisdom, academic rigor, and visionary perspective on the future of medicine. His work challenges physicians and healthcare systems to balance technological advancement with the timeless human values of presence, compassion, and meaning.

www.ingramcontent.com/pod-product-compliance
Lightning Source LLC
LaVergne TN
LVHW022057200926
848481LV00003B/948